# PLOTINUS AND NEOPLATONISM

# Plotinus
# and Neoplatonism

*An Introductory Study*

PHILIPPUS VILLIERS PISTORIUS

*M.A., B.D. (Stellenbosch); D.Litt. (Pretoria); D.Litt. et Phil. (Leiden);*
*Professor of Hellenistic and Patristic Greek at the University of Pretoria*

BOWES & BOWES
CAMBRIDGE

*First published in 1952 by*
*Bowes & Bowes Publishers Limited, Cambridge*

Printed in Great Britain for Bowes & Bowes, Limited
by A. R. Mowbray & Co. Limited in the City of Oxford

# FOREWORD

THE terms of the grant made by the South African Council for Social Research preclude any lengthy discussion of the views held by other interpreters of Plotinus.

In this study I have come to the conclusion that a theistic interpretation of Plotinus is not only possible, but even inevitable. The view that the Ideal World is a graded triad, is, in my opinion, erroneous. I have found in the three hypostases of that Ideal World nothing more than three aspects of one Divine Being.

I have made use of the translation of Mackenna where the only difference between his translation and mine would have been a difference in wording. I have avoided Greek quotations in order to make the book available to a wider circle.

P. V. PISTORIUS

Opgedra aan professor

H. G. VILJOEN

van die Universiteit van Pretoria

## NOTE

Acknowledgment is made to the National Council for Social Research of the Department of Union Education, Pretoria, for financial assistance in the publication of this work.

Opinions expressed and conclusions reached by the writer are his sole responsibility, and can in no way be regarded as representing the views of the National Council for Social Research.

# CONTENTS

# CONTENTS

# PLOTINUS AND NEOPLATONISM

## INTRODUCTION

TO understand Plotinus is difficult; to give a systematic account of his philosophy is well-nigh impossible. Even when one reads the works of Plotinus himself, one comes to the reluctant conclusion that the philosopher failed in his attempt to transfer thoughts into words. The insuperable obstacle that confronted him was language, the eternal enemy of idealistic philosophy. Language was evolved from and adapted to the things that are the objects of sense-perception, and it is one of the basic standpoints of Idealism that the world of sense has merely a second-rate reality, and that true existence is the prerogative of the unperceived world of concepts. It follows logically that when Idealism is constrained to give expression to that world of concepts in words based on material things, the attempt is bound to be a failure.

That has been my main difficulty in this commentary on Plotinus, whom I regard as one of the greatest idealists of all time, and perhaps the most profound philosopher of the Greek world. We may unreservedly reject the opinion that Plotinus was a product of oriental mysticism. We know from his works that he was conversant with the main truths of oriental thought, and, although nothing is known of his nationality, we know from Eunapius that he was born in Egypt. But whatever land gave him birth, I hope to prove in these pages that he was the spiritual child of Plato, and as the apostle of Platonism, reached heights unknown to his predecessors.

My method will be, in the first place, to give a brief summary of the Neo-Platonistic system, and only then to deal with the whole system in a more detailed and logical sequence. The apparent repetition in this method is unfortunately a necessity. The system of Plotinus is a unity, and it is very difficult to discuss one aspect of that system without in some way presupposing a knowledge of other aspects. The *Enneads*, as we know, do not present a systematic treatment of Plotinian thought. Even the opening sentences of the work presuppose a knowledge of the whole system. Plotinus certainly was no lucid teacher, and our introductory summary will have to serve as a *vade mecum* in respect of matters to which, although as yet unexplained, I shall perforce refer from time to time.

The central thought in the system of Plotinus is the existence of an ideal world, which is not only the prototype of the world of sense but is also the ultimate reality. Although this ideal world cannot be perceived by the senses, it can, with certain reservations, be the object of study. In this ideal world we find three essential principles or hypostases. In the first place there is the One or the Good, whom Plotinus regards as the inexpressible principle, beyond human reasoning, the stream which is its own source. It surpasses all known qualities. We cannot even say of it that it exists. As the source of all existence it must of necessity surpass existence.

The second hypostasis is the Intellectual-Principle, or the Nous. Through it we know of the One. This Nous shares certain qualities with the ideal world of Plato, although, as I hope to prove, it far excels the Platonic world of ideas. It is the image of the One, although it presents a deviation from the stern simplicity of the One, because in a certain respect it betrays a dualism. It is the first hypostasis of which we can say that it thinks, while the One is beyond thought, even beyond self-thought, as it is beyond all other possible predicates. But the thoughts of the Nous are not mediate or discursive—it is its own object of thought.

It is therefore at the same time intellection and the object of intellection. It is νοῦς and νοητά. And that is its dualistic aspect, a dualism that exists merely in the logical distinction between thought and its object. I say logical, because there is in reality no dualism. Thought and object of thought are identical in the Nous.

The third hypostasis is Soul, or the Principle of Life. It is the image of the Nous as the Nous is the Image of the One. This Soul is the author of the visible world, although in the case of man, the thinker, there are also certain other points of contact with the two first hypostases. All three hypostases are present in man, although they are not always revealed in all men. The human soul, in a certain sense, is the centre of the Plotinian system; it presents a point of contact with the visible world of sense and also with the ultimate reality.

The visible world was not created in time. Time is a concomitant of the visible world, not its matrix. The universe is the result of the action or rather the contemplation of the ultimate reality on matter. It is the reflection of the image of God, but not a perfect image, because it is material. The universe is therefore dependent on God, not only for its creation but also for its continued existence.

The substratum, or matter, is void of quality. ~~I believe that Plotinus regarded it as space~~—the void. It has nothing in common with what we regard as matter. To us, matter is the tangible, the visible something that is the basis of the visible world, and it has qualities—mass, form and volume. For Plotinus it is merely a logical abstraction. It is poverty-stricken and without predicate, and only by a pseudo-conception is it endowed with qualities by the contemplation of the ultimate reality. It is the invisible mirror, Plotinus says, which in an imperfect way reflects the ideal world, and because the ideal world, like the mirror, is invisible, we in our ignorance believe that the visible reflection, the world of sense, is reality.[1]

In the first tractate of the fifth *Ennead* Plotinus introduces us in a very clear way to the study of the three hypostases which comprise the God of Neo-Platonism. His reasoning is that before we dare seek after God, and before we undertake to probe into His being and character, we must be convinced that He is not totally strange to us.

'The seeker is Soul and it must start from a true notion of the nature and quality by which soul may undertake the search; it must study itself in order to learn whether it has the faculty for the inquiry, the eye for the object proposed, whether in fact we ought to seek; for if the object is alien the search must be futile, while if there is relationship the solution of our problem is at once desirable and possible'.[2]

In his answer to this question Plotinus granted the fact that man was indeed in a certain sense estranged from God. 'What can it be that has brought the souls to forget the father, God, and, though members of the Divine and entirely of that world, to ignore at once themselves and It?'[3] The Higher Beings are exalted above space and time. Movement, change, divisibility and similar matters are things to which man is prone as a result of his intimate contact with matter, but in reality they are strange to his true nature, although it may easily happen that he becomes so involved in the things of this world that the categories of the Higher Beings become strange to him, and can no longer be the objects of his thoughts.

The result is that man does not realize his own divinity. Things that are strange to our true nature become the objects of our love, and that very fact is the true cause of our sense of inferiority. To rectify this, the soul must follow a double path. 'A double discipline must be applied if human beings in this pass are to be reclaimed, and brought back to their origins, lifted once more towards the Supreme and One and First. This is the discipline declaring the dishonour of the object which the soul holds here in honour . . .; the second teaches and recalls to the soul the character of its race and worth'.[4]

In the second paragraph of this tractate Plotinus proceeds to prove that the soul is indeed divine. At this stage I will do no more than point out that the immortality of the soul is one of the fundamental principles of Plotinus, although, as we shall see later, it is doubtful whether by that he means the immortality of the individual human soul. And by virtue of the divine nature of the soul, man is entitled to seek and find God. 'The Soul once seen to be thus precious, thus divine, you may hold the faith that by its possession you are already nearing God: in the strength of this power make upwards towards Him: at no great distance you must attain: there is not much between'.[5]

But who and what is this God who is the fitting object of human desire? Plotinus sees in the multiversal nature of the universe an indication of the existence of a transcendent Unity. 'Before the manifold, there must be the One, that from which the manifold rises: in all numerical series, the unit is the first. But—we will be answered—for number, well and good, since the suite makes a compound; but in the real beings why must there be a unit from which the multiplicity of entities shall proceed? Because, failing such a unity, the multiplicity would consist of disjointed items, each starting at its own distinct place and moving accidentally to serve a total'.[6]

In other words, from the teleology of the universe Plotinus postulates a governing unity, which in some way must be the author or basis of all existence.

That this One cannot be Thought or Nous, is clear. The purest form of thought exists where the thinker and the object of thought are identical, but even the Intellectual-Principle, in which thought and thinker are indeed identical, cannot be called a simplex, because there is a distinction, even though it may merely be a logical distinction, between νοῦς and νοητά, or between thinker and object of thought. The distinction that Plotinus makes between this Intellectual-Principle and the One is sometimes very slight, and there is the danger that one may overlook the existence of the One.

He sometimes speaks of the Intellectual Principle as in fact a simplex. 'Does it all come down, then, to one phase of the self contemplating another phase? That would be a case of knower distinguished from known, and would not be self-knowing . . . The object known must be identical with the knowing act, the Intellectual-Principle, therefore, identical with the Intellectual Realm'.[7] The distinction is merely logical. The Intellectual-Principle and the Intellectual Realm are one, but the latter is a multiplicity because it is the prototype of the visible universe—the Platonic world of ideas, where everything indeed leads to unity, although the starting point of that road is multiplicity.

This ultimate Being, then, beyond the Intellectual-Principle and beyond thought, Plotinus calls the One. And even then the philosopher qualifies his statement. He is the One or the First, but not in the sense that He is the first in a numeric series. 'And this name, the One, contains really no more than the negation of plurality . . . If we are led to think positively of the One, name and thing, there would be more truth in silence: the designation, a mere aid to inquiry, was never intended for more than a preliminary affirmation of absolute simplicity to be followed by the rejection of even that statement'.[8]

One would be tempted to attribute to Plotinus the idea of J. Scotus Erigena, who called God the Nihil, but that would be to miss the Plotinian distinction between 'not something', and 'nothing'. God can definitely not be 'Something'. He is the source of everything and therefore apart. The source of all the 'some-things' cannot himself be 'something'. He cannot be identical with that of which He is the source.

But that does not mean that He is 'nothing'. In the same way that He cannot be the 'thing' of which He is the source, He cannot be the negation or the opposite of the thing of which He is the source. We have already seen that the Plotinian God, in his character as the One, cannot be the object of thought because thought involves a logical dualism. But would we on that account call Him 'thoughtless'? He is exalted above thought, not deprived of it.

The same distinction is drawn by Leighton,[9] who says that, because God is the source of our values, He must of necessity be higher than our values but not without them. Our personality is based on God, but we cannot speak of God as a person, because He transcends personality.

It is certain that Plotinus has difficulty in expressing his thoughts in words, but what he means is clear enough. Far from implying that God is 'nothing', he implies that God is the measure of all things. 'The One does not bear to be numbered in with anything else, with a one or a two or any such quantity; it refuses to take number because it is measure and not the measured; it is no peer of other entities to be found among them; for thus it and they alike would be included in some container, and this would be its prior, the prior it cannot have'.[10] In other words, when we say that God is the One, we merely deny that He is the many. Because we feel that the multiplicity around us demands an absolute unity transcending it, and because even the Intellectual-Principle, or ideal world, does not exhibit this unity, we postulate a super-unity, but apart from denying that He is the many or the second or something else, we must be silent.

We may not even say that God is called the One because He is the totality of the universe. He is not that totality. Men like Vacherot find a pantheistic character in the One of Plotinus. When later we deal with the question of immanence and transcendence we shall have the opportunity to examine this statement, but here we can say that Plotinus categorically denies it. 'The Unity cannot be the total of things, for so its oneness is annulled'.[11]

In conclusion we can say that Plotinus attempts to explain the universe through a unity, but the human intellect is powerless to qualify this unity. He says: 'What then must the unity be and what nature is left for it? No wonder that to state it is not easy; even Being and Form are not easy, though we have a way, an approach through the Ideas. The soul or mind reaching towards the formless finds itself incompetent to grasp where nothing bounds it, or to take impression where the impinging reality is diffuse; in sheer dread of holding to nothingness, it slips away. The state is painful; often it seeks relief by retreating from all this vagueness to the region of sense, there to rest as on solid ground, just as the sight distressed by the minute rest with pleasure on the bold. Soul must see its own way; this is by coalescence, unification; but in seeking thus to know the Unity it is prevented by that very unification from recognizing that it has found. It cannot distinguish itself from the object of this intuition. None-the-less, this is our resource if our philosophy is to give us knowledge of the Unity'.[12]

# I

# THE NATURE OF THE ONE

*The One as the Undefined*

The scholiasts have said that God has His centre everywhere and His circumference nowhere. That is also true of the One. He is the undefined. He transcends the universe.[13] The maker of all must have a self-sufficing existence outside of all things.[14] The result is that we cannot name Him. We cannot know Him, because knowledge implies limits to the thing that is known, and the One has no limits. To say 'I know God' is for Plotinus a contradiction in terms. If He were known, He would not be God.

And not only can we not know Him in his fullness, but we are not even able to make any satement concerning Him. 'The One is in truth above all statement: any affirmation is of a thing; but the all-transcending, resting above even the most august Divine Mind, possesses, alone of all, true being, and is not a thing among things; we can give no name to it that would imply predication: we can but try to indicate, in our feeble way, something concerning it: when in our perplexity we object, "Then it is without self-perception, without self-consciousness, ignorant of itself"; we must remember that we have been considering it only in its opposites'.[15]

Plotinus very clearly stated the truth that the universe cannot limit God. It cannot be said of God that He is in the universe. 'The Authentic is contained in nothing, since nothing existed before it; of necessity anything coming after it must, as a first condition of existence, be contained by this All . . . It is our way to limit Being to the sense-known and therefore to think of omnipresence in terms of the concrete; in our overestimate of the sensible, we question how that other nature can reach over such vastness; but our great is small, and this, small to us, is great'.[16] And because the One is omnipresent in the sense that it has no magnitude, 'it is not merely present everywhere but in addition it is nowhere-present'.[17]

Inge thinks that the One can easily be confused with Matter in the system of Plotinus, but the apparent similarity is so superficial that nobody need fall into that error. Both the One and Matter are undefined: of neither can we state any predicate. But the difference is clear. The One is undefined because it transcends all predication. As the source of all qualities it transcends quality. But Matter in the Plotinian system is the negation of all reality. It does not transcend definition; it lacks definition. The point will be clarified in our treatment of Matter.

## The One as Unknowable

It is clear that this transcendent Being cannot be grasped by the human intellect. Its very unity precludes knowledge of it. 'How, then, do we ourselves come to be speaking of it? No doubt we deal with it, but we do not state it; we have neither knowledge nor intellection of it'.[18] Human reason works through analysis and synthesis. There is nothing that we can know immediately by the aid of our discursive reason. Even the most simple statement presupposes analysis. When I state that a particular horse is white, I have in fact already isolated a certain number of essential horse-qualities, and these qualities have in my reasoning been compared with similar qualities in similar animals which I have come to recognize as horses. The resultant similarity between these qualities has caused me to call the particular white animal a horse. The same process takes place in connection with the concept 'white'.

But if we know only through analysis it follows that we cannot know a simplex like the One. We could, of course, say that there are many simple objects which we know, but there is no simplex except the One. Even the most elementary concept or object is, in fact, the product of many complex factors. It has qualities; and through qualities we know. But the One has no qualities.

On the other hand, we must guard against the mistaken conclusion of Caird[19] who states that Plotinus was an agnostic. The organ of human knowledge is the discursive reason, and had we no other means of acquiring knowledge, we could not have known God. But Plotinus states very clearly that we are not void of God. 'We do not, it is true, grasp it by knowledge, but that does not mean that we are utterly void of it; . . . unable to state it, we may still possess it . . . Those divinely possessed and inspired have at least the knowledge that they hold some greater thing within them though they cannot tell what it is. It is above reason, mind and feeling; conferring these powers, not to be confounded with them'.[20] When we deal with Plotinian psychology we will see that

Plotinus saw in the human psyche three phases or aspects—the animal or vegetative phase, the reasonable or human phase, and the divine or intuitive phase. It is this last phase of the human soul that is the organ by which we know God. These matters will be dealt with at length in our treatment of the religious application of the system of Plotinus, but at this stage the following passage from the *Enneads* will illustrate our meaning:

'At the moment of touch there is no power whatever to make any affirmation; there is no leisure; reasoning on the vision is for afterwards. We may know we have had the vision when the Soul has suddenly taken light. This light is from the Supreme and is the Supreme; we may believe in the Presence when, like that other god on the call of a certain man, He comes bringing light: the light is the proof of the advent. Thus the Soul unlit remains without that vision; lit, it possesses what it sought. And this is the true end set before the Soul, to take that light, to see the Supreme by the Supreme and not by the light of any other principle—to see the Supreme which is also the means to the vision; for that which illumines the Soul is that which it is to see, just as it is by the sun's own light that we see the sun'.[21]

## The One and Being, Thought and Purpose

Can we say of the One that it has Being? In other words, does it exist? Plotinus apparently denies it. 'It follows that the First must be without form, and, if without form, then it is no Being; Being must have some definition and therefore be limited; but the First cannot be thought of as having definition and limit, for thus it would be not the source but the particular item indicated by the definition assigned to it. If all things belong to the produced, which of them would you say belongs to the Supreme? Not included among them, this can be described only as transcending them: but they are Being and the Beings; it therefore transcends Being'.[22]

Is God, then, the Nihil? Is Plotinus an oriental philosopher whose mysticism ends in metaphysical nihilism? To draw this conclusion would be to confuse the concepts 'Reality' and 'Being'. The reality of an entity is in converse relation to the measure of its being or existence. A particular stone exists, but the measure of its reality is no more than the slight measure proper to inanimate objects. Reality is an attribute of the universal, not of the particular. We have in a certain sense already dealt with this matter in our distinction between 'nothing' and 'no thing'.

What, then, is the meaning of Plotinus? The One is the ultimate Reality—all other things are real only in so far as they share in the One. He is the source, and because He is the source, He is a simplex, in which the multiplicity of the universe finds its co-ordinating factor. He has no quality because He is the source of all qualities and therefore transcends quality. In the same way, 'being' or 'existence' is a secondary of which the One is the transcendent source, and therefore the One cannot have being as a quality.

But we cannot on that ground say that the One is a nihil. The nihil is that which is without being in the sense that it is deprived of it, but, as the source of existence or being, the One cannot be deprived of it. It is not the infra-red of being, but the ultra-violet. May I state it as follows? His 'Being' is higher than being, but because the human intellect cannot conceive of a higher being than being, we must be silent in our attempt to qualify his 'Being'. Plotinus himself tells us that we can know the One only through his opposites.

In the same way the One is also exalted above thought. It may be that common sense would here call a halt. Surely God thinks!

But this objection falls away for two reasons. In the first place Plotinus points out very clearly that the One must be an absolute simplex. Such a simplex cannot be the subject or object of thought, not even self-thought, because even there we have a duality between the thinker and the object of thought.

'If we allow intellection in it we make it indigent as far as intellection is concerned . . . The wholly simplex and veritable self-sufficing can be lacking at no point: self-intellection begins in that principle which, secondarily self-sufficing, yet needs itself and therefore needs to know itself . . . Consciousness is an act exercised upon a manifold . . . If the agent says no more than "I am a being", it speaks as a discoverer of the extern'.[23]

In another tractate Plotinus says: 'If the Good is simplex and without need, it can neither need the intellective act nor possess what it does not need: it will therefore not have intellection'.[24]

'The multiple must be always seeking its identity, desiring self-accord and self-awareness: but what scope is there within what is an absolute unity in which to move towards its identity? . . . There exists the Good; . . . and the intellective act may be defined as a movement towards the Good in some being that aspires toward it . . . Hence the Authentic Good has no need of intellection since itself and nothing else is good'.[25]

In the second place we must point out that the One is God, but not the whole Godhead. I believe, and in a later chapter I hope to prove, that the three hypostases of Plotinus form an absolute unity, where each hypostasis is but an aspect of the whole. It need therefore not appear strange to state that the One has no thought.

I certainly do not agree with Inge[26] who states that Plotinus ascribes a kind of exalted self-thought to the One. Inge says: 'He (the One) has self-discernment, which implies a sort of self-consciousness'. No wonder that on the next page Inge confesses that he cannot agree with Plotinus in this respect. 'The criticism will certainly be made that Plotinus, after protesting that nothing can be said of the Absolute, tells us a good deal about it or him, investing him in fact with the attributes of a personal God. We must not say that he thinks, and yet he comprehends everything'.

It would have been very difficult to meet this criticism, were it not for the fact that it is based on an irrelevant passage (VI. 7, 16). Plotinus, in that section, is not speaking of the One at all, but deals with the Intellectual-Principle, the Nous, and its indwelling in the One. Self-discernment is indeed, according to Plotinus, an attribute of that Nous, but nowhere does the philosopher ascribe anything like thought or self-discernment to the One. Eucken is guilty of the same error.[27]

Plotinus has a similar answer to the related question whether the One is free and has volition. The whole problem is dealt with in VI. 8, 1–21, where he speaks of free-will and the will of the One.

Freedom, he says, is ascribed to a human being when action is in accord with the will of the agent. But sometimes we act in accordance with volition without being free. We may, for example, be under the influence of a narcotic. 'If rage or desire implied freedom we must allow freedom to animals, infants, maniacs, the distraught, the victims of malpractice producing uncontrollable delusions'.[28] To be free, an action must also be the result of correct thought, and even then there is the proviso that such thought must have as its basis correct knowledge. Acts committed under the influence of desire or any other emotion are thus clearly excluded from the category of free acts. Only they are free whose acts are in no way influenced by the body, and only they whose volition is determined by their relation to the Intellectual-Principle, are not so influenced. Plotinus speaks of them as σπουδαίαι ψυχαί. Ficinus translates the phrase by *animae probrae*, and as we shall see later the meaning is very near to that of μύστης or ἐπόπτης, one who has been admitted to the highest grade of knowledge of the divine.

But is all this applicable to the One? Can the attribute freedom be applied to the One in the same way as it is applied to human beings? Man is no simplex. Consequently even his free actions are pre-determined by his environment, and that environment very often stands in sharp contrast to the person concerned. For instance, a brave man would very rarely desire the circumstances which form the background to any particular act of bravery on his part. Free acts, according to Plotinus, are those acts which strive after the Good, the One; and a person whose desires are for the Good would not desire war or violence, although, should those circumstances occur, he would perform brave acts of his own volition. Such free acts of bravery would in that case be free in a limited sense only, because they are pre-determined by environment and external factors.

There can actually be no absolute freedom in the case of an act. Later we shall see that Plotinus ascribes acts only to lower beings; an act is no more than an imperfect form of 'contemplation' which is the 'act' of the Higher Beings. But even contemplation cannot be free when it is directed towards external things. The act, or rather the contemplation of the Intellectual-Principle, is free, because, although it is directed towards the One, the One is not external in relation to the Intellectual-Principle—the two are the same Godhead, although they are different phases of that Godhead.

'In a principle, act and essence must be free. No doubt Intellectual-Principle itself is to be referred to a yet higher; but this higher is not extern to it; Intellectual-Principle is within the Good; possessing its own good in virtue of that indwelling, much more will it possess freedom and self-disposal which are sought only for the sake of the good. Acting towards the Good, it must all the more possess self-disposal, for by that act it is directed towards the Principle from which it proceeds, and thus its act is self-centred and must entail its very greatest good'.[29]

Freedom in the case of the Intellectual-Principle is consequently not in the same category as freedom when applied to a human being. In the one case it is pure, in the other it is imperfect. The

Intellectual-Principle has no environment to determine it. It thinks, but it thinks itself. It has volition, but it wills itself or, to state the same fact differently, it wills the One or the Good. Consequently it is free in an absolute sense.

But what about the One? Later I shall attempt to prove that the One is the transcendent phase of the Godhead. Can we speak of freedom and volition in connection with the One? Plotinus answers the first question in the affirmative, but not the second. Let us take the question of thought as our parallel. The Intellectual-Principle thinks itself as object of its own thought, but the One does not think, because thinking involves a duality. In the same way the Intellectual Principle wills the One, and even if those two entities are the same, the activity of volition is still a proof of duality which would be foreign to a simplex. Apart from that, volition is an activity directed towards the One. Why, then, would the One will something? Desire is an implied want, even when such desire is free. And because the One has no want, it cannot desire anything. Everything moves toward the One, in other words, wills the One. But the One wills nothing, because it is self-sufficing. In an earlier *Ennead* Plotinus says: 'The multiple must be always seeking its own identity, desiring self-accord and self-awareness: but what scope is there within what is an absolute unity in which to move towards its identity? . . . It holds its identity in its very essence and is above consciousness and all intellective act . . . The intellective act may be defined as a movement towards the Good in some being that aspires towards it. Hence the Authentic Good has no need of intellection since itself and nothing else is its good'.[30]

Nevertheless the One is free. Freedom, according to Plotinus, is the absence of determining externa. Our freedom is never absolute, because we are always under the determining influence of an environment, and therefore freedom, when applied to the One, would be a totally different matter. 'How, then, can the lord of all that august sequence—the first in place, that to which all else strives to mount, all dependent upon it and taking from it their powers even to this power of self-disposal—how can This be brought under the freedom belonging to you and to me? . . . It is rash thinking drawn from another order that would imagine a First Principle to be controlled by a manner of being imposed from without, void therefore of freedom or self-disposal, acting or refraining under compulsion . . . This state of freedom belongs in the absolute degree to the Eternals in right of that eternity and to other things in so far as without hindrance they possess or pursue the Good which, standing above them all, must manifestly be the only good they can reasonably seek'.[31]

Plotinus no doubt realized the dangerous implications of this thesis. To say that God has no environment, that there are no *externa* in relation to Him, is either to deny the existence of the universe or else to deny any relation between God and universe. The first alternative is patently impossible. The second would expose the philosopher to the criticism that his conception of the deity approaches that of a Para-Brahm, so transcendent that man can never reach it.

What answer would Plotinus give to this criticism? There is, of course, the natural reply that the One is beyond human conception. Apparent contradictions in our attempted definition of Him are therefore unavoidable. 'But this Unoriginating, what is it? We can but withdraw, silent, hopeless, and search no further. What can we look for when we have reached the furthest? Every enquiry aims at a first and, that attained, rests. Besides, we must remember that all questioning deals with the nature of a thing, its quality, its cause or its essential being. In this case the being—in so far as we can use the word—is knowable only by its sequents: the question as to cause asks for a principle beyond, but the principle of all has no principle: the question as to quality would be looking for an attribute in that which has none: the question as to nature shows only that we must ask nothing about it but merely take it into the mind if we may, with the knowledge gained that nothing can be permissibly connected with it. The difficulty this principle presents to our mind in so far as we can approach to conception of it may be exhibited thus: We begin by posing space, a place, a Chaos; into this existing container, real or fancied, we introduce God and proceed to enquire: we ask, for example, whence and how He comes to be there: we investigate the presence and quality of the newcomer projected into the midst of things here from some height or depth. But the difficulty disappears if we eliminate all space before we attempt to conceive God. He must not be set in anything either as enthroned in eternal immanence or as having made some entry into things: He is to be conceived as existing alone, in that existence which the necessity of discussion forces us to attribute to Him, with space and all the rest as later than Him—space latest of all. Thus we conceive as far as we may, the spaceless; we abolish the notion of any environment: we circumscribe Him with no limit; we attribute no extension to Him; He has no quality since no shape, even shape Intellectual. He holds no relationship but exists in and for Himself before anything is'.[32]

Plotinus' conception of the One very definitely precludes all logical determination of the One as a separate entity. The One is literally unthinkable, because, were it thinkable, that simplex would cease to be a simplex in so far as it becomes the object of thought. I believe that all attempts on our part to reconcile the theses of Plotinus with the conception of the One as the Godhead, must ultimately land us in a maze of logical contradictions. I hope, later on in this work, to solve the problem by attempting to prove that the One is no *deus totus*, but nothing more than the transcendent aspect of the Godhead. It were vain, therefore, at this point to attempt to absolve Plotinus from a charge of deistic tendencies.

In conclusion, then, we say that the One does not possess volition, but that He is nevertheless free. Plotinus makes it clear, however, that freedom is not an attribute of the One. The freedom of the One must be understood in the negative sense that there is no determining factor in respect of Him. The One is free because there is no environment. Plotinus says: 'It is not, in our view, as an attribute that this freedom is present in the First. In the light of free acts, from which we eliminate the contraries, we recognize there self-determination, self-directed, and, failing more suitable terms, we apply to it the lesser terms brought over from lesser things and so tell it as best we may'.[33]

## The One and Goodness

Very often in the *Enneads* the One is called the Good. But just as the names, the First, or the One, do not postulate a positive statement in connection with the One, so also Plotinus has nothing positive to say when he calls Him the Good. 'Whatever may be said to be in need, is in need of a good and a preserver. Nothing can therefore be good to the One. Neither can it have will to anything. It is a Beyond-Good, not even to itself a good but to such beings only as may be of quality to have part with it'.[34]

The meaning is clear. He describes the One as the cause and then qualifies his statement by saying that it is the first cause of all things, and yet in another sense it is not the first cause, because it stands in no relation to them. In the same way it is his standpoint that the One is good in the sense that He is the transcendent source of our ethical values, but that we would not be justified in attributing goodness to Him as a predicate. 'Just as the goodness of the Good is essential and not the outgrowth of some prior substance, so the Unity of the One is its essential. When we speak of the One and when we speak of the Good we must recognize an Identical Nature: we must affirm that they are the same—not, it is true, as venturing any predication with regard to that hypostasis but simply as indicating it to ourselves in the best terms we find'.[35] Any attribute of predicate we find by conceptual comparison of existing entities, and the One transcends all existence. Therefore He can have no predicate, not even the predicate 'good'.

This does not mean that the One is not good. The same arguments are valid here as in the case of knowledge or self-knowledge in the One. 'This absence of self-knowing does not import ignorance; ignorance is of something outside—a knower ignorant of a knowable—but in the Solitary there is neither knowing nor anything unknown.'[36] Plotinus practically repeats this reasoning in dealing with the 'goodness' of the One. 'This Principle', he says, 'is not to be identified with the good of which it is the source; it is good in the unique mode of being the Good above all that is good'. And in the previous *Ennead* he says: 'It is the Good to the universe if only in this way, that towards it all things have their being, all dependent on it, each in its mode, so that thing rises above thing in goodness according to its possession of authentic being'.

Eventually, therefore, everything exists by virtue of the One, and what we call goodness is no more than the degree of participation in the One. The One itself, as source of all goodness, must transcend that attribute.

## Space and the One

One of the most important questions in connection with the One is the problem of its immanence or its transcendence in relation to the universe, and the problem is not made easier by the apparently contradictory words of Plotinus in this respect. No wonder that modern commentators are practically unanimous in their criticism of Plotinus on this point. Caird[37]—if I may be permitted to select only one example—says: 'The One is an exclusive unity—and is yet the source from which everything flows. These two aspects of the One are not reconciled in Plotinus, and he hides the difficulty of reconciling them by alternating between the language of exact thought and the language of imagination'. Other commentators like Grandgeorge,[38] Eucken,[39] and Inge[40] in the main voice the same doubts.

This misunderstanding of Plotinus is probably due to two causes. In the first place there is the relation of the three hypostases to one another. If the three are apart and if, as is popularly supposed, we have a graded triad in the system of Plotinus, I cannot see how the philosopher can be absolved from the criticism that his philosophy rests on a dualism. I hope to deal with this point later in detail.

In the second place, we must remember that immanence and transcendence need not necessarily be mutually exclusive. Leighton[41] says that God is transcendent because He is the basis and source of our values. But if He is the source of our values, He is naturally immanent in our values. He cannot be transcendent without being immanent. All our values point to God as the source, the unifying principle; and the *Enneads* of Plotinus teach the same lesson.

Must we, then, conclude that the One is also immanent, as He is transcendent? This question is the crux of the system of Plotinus. Modern commentators seem to find no decisive answer in the *Enneads*. Apparently Plotinus insists, on the one hand, that the One is only transcendent, that it is far removed from all human qualities and concepts in its lonely majesty, while, on the other hand, critics apparently seem to find proof in the *Enneads* that it is the source from which everything flows.

I shall answer the question as follows: the One, in its character as the One, is transcendent, but the Neoplatonic Godhead, which includes the One, the Intellectual-Principle and the Soul or the Principle of Life, is immanent and transcendent. No Godhead can be anything else, and the arguments of the deist or the pantheist are in fact no more than a series of contradictions. If we insist on postulating a God who is only transcendent we must logically arrive at the Indian concept of a Nihil, a Para-Brahm, and conversely, the only deity of whom we say say it is exclusively immanent, is the negative concept of atheistic pantheism. And in neither case is there an answer to the question of the authorship of the universe.

The transcendent deity of the deist would not have cared to create, the immanent god of pantheism would have been powerless to do so.

It is interesting, in the light of this question, to see what Plotinus tells us of that transcendent being in its relation to the world and to space. The most important passage is undoubtedly v. 3, 11:

'The Principle before all these principles is no doubt the first principle of the universe, but not as immanent: immanence is not for primal sources but for engendering secondaries; that which stands as primal source of everything is not a thing but is distinct from all things; it is not, then, a member of the total but earlier than all, earlier, thus, than the Intellectual-Principle—which in fact envelops the entire train of things. Thus we come, once more, to a Being above the Intellectual-Principle, and, since the sequent amounts to no less than the All, we recognize, again, a Being above the All'.

This passage speaks for itself. Perhaps the following two citations would be useful before I come to the apparently contradictory words of the philosopher.

'Thus the One is in truth beyond all statement: any affirmation is of a thing; but the all-transcending, resting above even the most august Divine Mind, possesses alone of all true being and is not a thing among things; we can give it no name because that would imply predication: we can try but to indicate, in our own feeble way, something, concerning it'.[42]

'Everything brought into being under some principle not itself is contained either within its maker or, if there is any intermediate, within that . . . firsts within prior-firsts and so thing within thing up to the very pinnacle of source. That source, having no prior, cannot be contained . . . Holding all—though itself nowhere held— it is omnipresent, for where its presence failed, something would elude its hold. At the same time, in the sense that it is nowhere held it is not present. Thus it is both present and not present; not present as not being circumscribed by anything; yet, as being utterly un- attached, not inhibited from presence at any point'.[43]

I have already stated that Plotinus apparently contradicts himself in this respect. The relation of the One to the universe is sometimes explained in such a way that it is difficult, if not impossible, to avoid the conclusion that the transcendence of the One is not absolute. The most glaring example I have found in v. 6, 3:

'This unity must be numbered as first before all and can be appre- hended only as solitary and self-existent. When we recognize it, resident among the mass of things, our business is to see it for what it is—present to the items but essentially distinguished from them'.

Mackenna,[44] in his introduction to his excellent translation of the works of Plotinus, points out that sometimes, when one of the three hypostases is definitely named, the entire context shows that the reference is not to the hypostasis named, but to the Triad collectively or to one of the two not named.

Can we explain away our difficulty in this way? I do not believe that it is possible, however tempting such an escape would be. The context of the passage in question raises the issue above all doubt. The One is meant, and no other entity.

But it is also clear that the passage lands us in difficulties. 'Resident among the mass of things . . . present to the items'— these words could only have been said of something immanent, not of an exclusively transcendent being.

I believe that the solution to the problem must be sought in the following direction. We have already seen that immanence and transcendence presuppose one another. We have also seen that in all the cited passages, with this one exception, Plotinus insists on the absolute transcendence of the One. But the One is not the Plotinian Godhead. I believe that the One is to Plotinus nothing more than the transcendent phase or aspect of the Godhead. By that Plotinus means that the One is the source of all reality. Our values are real in so far as they approach that source. That transcendent being is the *sine qua non* of all. 'If its fixed seat were shaken, all the rest would fall with the fall of their foundation and stay', says Plotinus.[45]

The One is exalted above the universe, but the universe nevertheless exists solely by virtue of the One. Is the One in everything? No, but everything is in Him. The degree in which any entity is in the One, decides the degree of reality of that entity. Notwithstanding, or rather, because of His transcendence, everything has a share in Him. He is not immanent in the universe. The universe is immanent in Him.

Plotinus did not possess, as we possess, a rich heritage of philosophical thought and phraseology. He struggled with a problem of which he could see the solution, although he was powerless to express it. But his meaning is quite clear. He says, for example, that the One is the source of the universe.

'Before the manifold, there must be the One, that from which the manifold rises . . . Because (failing such a unity) the multiplicity would consist of disjointed items, each starting at its own distinct place, and moving accidentally to serve a total'.[46]

The nature of the problem is clear. The One is transcendent and at the same time it must stand in a causal relation to the universe. I have already indicated the direction in which I think the reconciliation of these two divergent attributes should be sought, and before embarking on a detailed discussion, I shall make the following statement: In the first place, the three hypostases of the Neo-Platonic Godhead are not a gradation of three separate beings, as is generally believed, but a more intimate trinity than that of Christian theology, because neither the One, nor the Intellectual Principle, nor the Soul, can conceivably exist as independent and separate entities. Taken separately, they are little more than logical abstractions, and only when they are thought of as one Godhead, do they yield one of the richest and most logical conceptions of the ultimate reality ever found in any theological or philosophical system.

In the second place, I wish to say that unless this thesis is correct, the product of Plotinian thought is a coarse and irreconcilable dualism, clumsily held together, as Caird thinks, by the device of alternating between the language of exact thought and the language of imagination.

It is, of course, not possible for us at this stage to discuss in detail the Plotinian distinction between the three hypostases. I shall therefore do no more than prove that the One can have no separate being.

What has Plotinus told us about it? Merely that there is nothing to tell. It is a barren simplex which even includes the negation of the conception of unity. It is unthinkable, it has no existence, no thought, no volition. It is absolutely transcendent. It has no attribute. We dare not call it beautiful or good. It is a universal concept robbed of all its qualities. It is more universal than the highest idea in the scheme of Plato, because the ideas of Plato are reasonable and open to human understanding. The search after concepts is the task of discursive reasoning. Even the Platonic One, the absolute reality, is reached by discursive reasoning through the method of analysis and synthesis.

Plato blundered because he granted individual existence to universal concepts, but if the One of Plotinus is a separate entity, he sinned more in this respect than Plato.

But is it? The One is not Being. It does not exist. It is postulated as *causa efficax* of the universe just as the mathematician postulates a triangle, although a triangle as such does not exist. Or does it? Surely it exists only in such an intimate relation to tangible objects that, when abstracted from the tangible object, it ceases to exist. It is nothing more than a logical postulate which serves as a *sine qua non* for mathematical reasoning.

That, and nothing more, can be said of the One. It is deprived of all attributes, and consequently it can have no independent existence. It has no attributes. It is itself an attribute of the ultimate reality.

Were it true that Plotinus regarded the One as an independently existing divine principle, we would be justified in saying that the philosopher had, probably under the influence of oriental thought, created a deistic Para-Brahm, a god of no account, to whom we would not give respect, fear, love or hate, because in reality he would not exist for us. He would have no claim to our worship, because he would have been unconscious of worship. He is unconscious of us as he is apparently unconscious of himself. He would have been powerless to aid or harm us, because his barren transcendence forbids all contact with the outside world. No wonder that modern commentators regard the Intellectual-Principle as the Plotinian god, but that also is nothing more than half the truth. Even a superficial study of the *Enneads* would convince anybody that Plotinus actually speaks of the One as the Supreme Being.

But not the entire Godhead. In that case there would have been an absolute gulf between God and the universe. Contact would have been impossible. The One transcends all the categories of the visible and the invisible universe. Even thought, one of the highest categories, is strange to the One. Here, then, we would have had the final dualism, because not only would the gulf between God and the universe have been unbridged; a bridge would have been impossible. Logically we would not even have been able to say of the One that it transcends the universe, because transcendence presupposes immanence. Had the One been in the true sense transcendent with respect to the universe, the universe would have been logically immanent in the One. He would have been the basis, the final ground, of all our categories. Our thought, although God transcends thought, would have been immanent in Him because He is the source of it.

That is not the case in Plotinus. It is true that he says of the One that it is the source of everything, but as Stace[47] points out in his discussion of the One in Plato, the Absolute, to be a source, must be neither an abstract One, nor an abstract many. It must be a many-in-one. And the Plotinian One is a barren simplex. When Plotinus calls it the source of the universe, it follows that either Plotinus is guilty of self-contradiction, or otherwise our thesis is the correct explanation, namely that the One is an attribute of the Absolute, an aspect, namely its transcendence.

If we accept the view that the One is merely an aspect of the Godhead, our difficulties disappear automatically. In that case we refrain from passing final judgment on the Plotinian conception of God until such time that we will be in a position to take the other two hypostases or rather, aspects, into consideration, namely the Intellectual-Principle and the Soul.

We have therefore in the One an attribute of God. It is God seen in His transcendence and lonely majesty. God, in His character as the unthinkable Being, into Whose secrets the human intellect cannot probe, the Being who transcends being, into Whose presence we dare not go when our feet are shod with the sandals of human reason, the unapproachable Transcendence—that is the One.

But, it may be said, we have already pointed out that Plotinus, when he states that the One has no being, does not mean that the One is deprived of being. Surely, if it transcends being, it excels it and does not fall below it.

Precisely in that way, I believe, we can distinguish between the universal and the particular. In Christian theology it is believed that goodness is an attribute of God. We can say: God is goodness. But if goodness is an attribute, or shall we say, *merely* an attribute, of God, do we by that decrease its measure of reality? It does not exist apart from God. There is no separate entity called goodness. It is not the particular. It is the universal. It does not exist as the city of Cape Town exists or as I exist, but none the less the measure of its reality is so high that in the Platonic system it is the all-embracing Idea. Need we then object that by calling the Plotinian One an attribute of the Supreme Being, we decrease its glory and that our theory is inconsistent with the place which Plotinus gives to it? I do not think so.

I shall close this chapter by provisionally accepting, as a working hypothesis, the theory that the One has no separate being apart from the two other Plotinian hypostases, that it is the transcendent aspect of God, and that its transcendence can be logically, though not actually, distinguished from its immanence. That Plotinus himself does not attempt so to distinguish is shown by the fact that he does not succeed in separating the idea of teleology from the One, although, as we shall see later, the teleological aspect of God is the Intellectual Principle.

Our preliminary conclusions, then, are:

1. What Plotinus says of the One, excludes the possibility that it is an independent Being.

2. The One is therefore an aspect of God, namely his transcendence.

## Unity and Multiplicity

Inge[48] is right when he finds the centre of gravity of the Neoplatonic system in the Nous, but he is wrong when he states that the Intellectual-Principle, or as he calls it, the Spiritual World, is for Plotinus the ultimate reality. The Intellectual-Principle or Nous is no simplex. Although νοῦς and νοητά are one, there is the logical distinction between them, and Plotinus very clearly states that the ultimate reality must be an absolute simplex.

That is our problem. How can the One serve as the source of multiplicity, of which we have the initial stage in the logical duality of the Intellectual-Principle? This problem was the rock on which the metaphysical system of Plato foundered. It is true that Plato postulated ideas which were the archetypes of the visible world. But the teleological *modus quo* is not so postulated. How did the multiple emerge from the simple and the particular from the universal? There is certainly nothing intrinsically teleological in the ideas of Plato, just as there is nothing intrinsically comprehensive in his idea of the Good.

Plato tells us that they are archetypes. He also tells us that visible objects are the copies of those archetypes. But why should there be archetypes, and why copies? In vain do we attempt to find a satisfactory answer in Plato, and the fact that he produces God as a *deus ex machina* from nowhere to fashion matter into copies of the ideas, is a clear proof that Plato was confronted by an irreconcilable dualism.

The Absolute and the particular stand disconnected, and to connect them with the aid of a third entity, which he calls God, is to confess that they are incapable of being connected. Nor can Plato be absolved from the charge that he regarded his highest Idea, the

Good, as God, because that particular Idea is as powerless as the others. There is nothing in its nature to make it a creator.

How did Plotinus approach this problem? Much will depend on our answer to this question. Our estimation of the value of Plotinus as philosopher will to a large extent depend upon the answer to the question whether he succeeded in providing a logical bond between the Absolute and the particular. In other words, already in the One we must find the cause of the multiplicity of the universe. If Plotinus, like Plato, attempted to answer the question in the language of symbolism or by a *tertium quid*, we will be forced to come to the conclusion that he failed as Plato failed before him.

We must remember that the One is absolutely transcendent. Its lonely majesty excludes all contact with the universe. Surely that is proof enough that we are doomed to abide by a dualism?

Our problem is, of course, in the first place, the logical necessity in the relation of the Intellectual-Principle to the One, or, to state it more clearly, the question how the Intellectual-Principle emerged from the One. The Intellectual-Principle is, seen from the standpoint of the One, the first step towards multiplicity, and once that step is granted, the question of the emergence of the multiplicity in the visible universe becomes more easy.

We have already seen that the One is an absolute simplex, but that it is nevertheless the basis of our values. 'Because (failing such a unity) the multiplicity would consist of disjointed items, each starting at its own distinct place and moving accidentally to serve a total'.[49]

But, it will be said, here we have nothing more than an acknowledgement that the universe demands a unifying principle. That such a principle is inherent in our values, or, conversely, that our values are inherent in that unity, we see clearly from the following passage taken from the same tractate.

'We do not, it is true, grasp it by knowledge, but that does not mean that we are utterly void of it . . . unable to state it, we may still possess it . . . above reason, mind and feeling; conferring these powers, not to be confounded with them. Conferring—but how? As itself possessing them, or not? How can it convey what it does not possess, yet if it does possess, how is it a simplex? And if, again, it does not, how is it the source of the manifold? A single, unmanifold emanation we may very well allow—how even that can come from a pure unity may be a problem, but we may always explain it on analogy of the irradiation from a luminary—but a multitudinous production raises question.

'The explanation is, that what comes from the Supreme cannot be identical with it and assuredly cannot be better than it—what could be better than the One and the utterly Transcendent? The emanation, then, must be less good, that is to say, less self-sufficing; now what must that be which is less self-sufficing than the One? Obviously the Not-One, that is to say, multiplicity. But multiplicity striving towards unity; that is to say, a One-that-is-Many.

'All that is not One is conserved by virtue of the One, and from the One derives its characteristic nature: if it had not attained such unity as is consistent with being made up of multiplicity we could not affirm its existence: if we are able to affirm the nature of single things, this is in virtue of the unity, the identity even, which each of them possesses. But the all-transcendent, utterly void of multiplicity, has no mere unity of participation but is unity's self, independent of all else, as being that from which, by whatever means, all the rest take their degree of unity in their standing, near or far, towards it.

'In virtue of the unity manifested in its variety it exhibits, side by side, both an all-embracing identity and the existence of the secondary: all the variety lies in the midst of a sameness, and identity cannot be separated from diversity since all stands as one; each item in that content, by the fact of participating in life, is a One-many: for the item could not make itself manifest as a One-and-all.

'Only the transcendent can be that; it is the great beginning, and the beginning must be a really existent One, wholly and truly One, while its sequent, poured down in some way from the One, is all, a total which has participation in unity, and whose every member is similarly All and One.

'What then is the All? The total of which the Transcendent is the Source. But how? . . . The Transcendent would contain only the potentiality of the universe to come.'[50]

This passage which I have quoted *in extenso*, is, I think, conclusive. There cannot be a One which is not also a many. One may, of course, like Plotinus, abstract the Oneness of the ultimate reality and then call it the absolutely Transcendent. In the same way one may abstract the whiteness of an object and call it the absolutely white, shorn of all other qualities. But in neither case have we established a separate entity. We have merely abstracted an attribute of an entity. There cannot be an entity whiteness as there cannot be an entity, the Absolute One, shorn of all attributes. Nor can one evade the issue by giving negative attributes, because every negative implies an opposite positive. A One which is not also a many, is inconceivable. The One and the many presuppose one another. We cannot, in the fashion of the Eleatics, separate them, nor does Plotinus attempt to do so.

I have already shown that the One is not a separate entity. It is not the Godhead. It is nothing more than the transcendent aspect of that Godhead. The Plotinian Godhead is, as we shall see, the three aspects together—the One, the Intellectual Principle and the Soul, a One-in-Many. Abstract the oneness or the many-ness, if you wish, but still they presuppose one another. One cannot abstract length from an object and then state that the object so deprived is without length or the length without object.

Let us go back to Plotinus. 'The item could not make itself manifest as a One-and-all. Only the Transcendent can be that. It is the great beginning, while its sequent is a total. The Transcendent would contain the potentiality of the universe to come'.

In other words, the Ultimate Reality is a One-in-Many, containing in potentiality the universe. It is One, because in that Ultimate Reality, the multiversal universe finds its essential unity. But it is also the many, because the universe is included, potentially, in it. Then Plotinus abstracts the oneness and calls it the One, but even in that One there is the potential many. Why is it the One? Because it is the unifying principle of the multiplicity in the universe. It is an attribute, an aspect, of the Ultimate Reality, the One-in-many.

The standpoint of Plotinus is perfectly clear, and perfectly in accord with Idealistic thought. The temporal is immanent in the eternal. There is no clear line of demarcation between the Absolute and the Particular. God and his universe are one. Consequently we may not abstract some aspect of God and call that aspect the Deity. Had the One been the Godhead, the immanence of the temporal in the eternal would have been impossible. But God is not only the One. He is also the Intellectual Principle and the Soul. He is One-in-Many. We must think of Hegel and the very clear resemblance between him and Plotinus. God and His creation cannot be thought of separately.

## II

## THE INTELLECTUAL PRINCIPLE

WE have already discussed the problem of the One and multiplicity. What, then, is the relation of the One to the Intellectual Principle?

At this stage it must be pointed out that there can be no question of an earlier or a later in the sense that the Intellectual Principle at some period did not exist. Tertullian says: *Fuit tempus cum Deo filius non fuit*, and without claiming that Tertullian is representative of Christian thought in his time, we must remember that Plotinus was far in advance of certain contemporaneous thinkers. In *Ennead* II. 1, 1 we read: 'We hold that the ordered universe in its material mass has existed for ever and will for ever endure'. The visible universe, as we shall see later, is the product of the contemplation of the Intellectual Principle on Matter. It therefore follows that such a principle is co-eternal with the ordered universe. God and His creation, as we have already stated, are correlative.

Therefore, to speak of the origin of the Intellectual Principle from the One, is to speak of a logical, not a temporal sequence.

How did this emanation take place? Indirectly this question has to a certain extent already been dealt with in the previous chapter, and, to be correct, the relation of the Intellectual Principle to the One should be dealt with at the end and not at the beginning of the chapter dealing with the Intellectual-Principle. At this stage it will suffice to say that the lonely majesty of the One precludes the emergence of any other entity, unless the first two hypostases are regarded as different aspects of the same being.

What is the Intellectual Principle? Plotinus calls it οὐσία, νοῦς, νόησις and νοητά, but never πνεῦμα, a word which for him apparently had a Stoic and materialistic connotation. Mackenna translates the concept by 'Intellectual-Principle'. I have, on the whole, made use of that translation, although there is the objection to it that it wrongly gives the impression of discursive thought, which is strange to the second Plotinian hypostasis. Inge calls it 'spirit', as νοῦς, and 'Spiritual World,' as νοητά, and were it not for the pseudo-materialistic connotation of that word in modern Christian phraseology, it would have been a good rendering. What I mean is this: We speak of spirit as a particular entity, although not corporeal, whereas spirit should be the universal, not the particular. I am not even referring to ectoplasmic spirits! That, of course, would be the essence of materialism. The fact that the matter concerned is in this case presumably very subtle and thin reminds one of the justification by an unmarried mother for the illegitimate baby, namely that it was only a very small one! German scholars call it *das Denken*, which is clearly wrong, because it translates διάνοια and not νοῦς. Were it not too cumbersome one would be able to call it 'the immediately self-thinking and intuitively knowing, all-embracing and all-creating God'. And even that would be incomplete.

I have not the slightest doubt that the Intellectual Principle was the starting-point of the Plotinian system, or rather that the Intellectual-Principle is, on the whole, the God of Plotinus. The One is for him a logical postulate as the unifying principle, while the Soul is the link between the Intellectual-Principle and the visible world. Inge[51] calls it the Neo-Platonic God, and we can accept that if we remember at the same time that the Intellectual-Principle becomes as barren a concept as the One, if it is viewed as an independent entity. Plotinus was an idealist, and as such he followed Plato in his belief that there was an ideal archetype of the visible universe. But he did not, like Plato, reach that world by the ladder of concepts. For Plato the ideas were knowable by the discursive reason. Even the highest idea, the archetype or idea of ideas, could be reached by the process of human thought. Not so Plotinus. He does not go from the visible to the invisible, from the particular to the universal, but from the universal to the particular. The Intellectual-Principle or the world of ideas, is for him the self-apparent ultimate reality and it needs no proof.

What is the content of this Intellectual-Principle? It consists of thought and the object of that thought, but the two are identical. There is only a logical distinction between νοῦς and νοητά. This νοητά or as Inge calls it, the Spiritual World, is nothing else than the ideas of Plato, shorn of their contradictions. Plotinus says: 'Now comes the question what sort of thing does the Intellectual Principle see in seeing the Intellectual Realm and what in seeing itself? We are not to look for an Intellectual realm reminding us of the colour or shape to be seen on material objects: the intellectual antedates all such things; and even in our sphere the production is very different from the Reason-Principle in the seeds from which is is produced. The seed principles are invisible and the beings of the Intellectual even more characteristically so; the Intellectuals are of one same nature with the Intellectual Realm'.[52]

The meaning is clear. The νοητά are the ideal archetypes—we have here a teleological entity. Of what are they the archetypes?

'This universe is a living thing capable of including every form of life; but its Being and its modes are derived from elsewhere; that source is traced back to the Intellectual-Principle. It follows that the all-embracing archetype is in the Intellectual-Principle, which, therefore, must be an Intellectual Kosmos, that indicated by Plato in the phrase, the *living existent* . . . All, then, that is present in the sense-realm comes from the Supreme. But what is not present as Idea, does not. Thus of things conflicting with nature, none is There. The inartistic is not contained in the arts; lameness not in the seed; for a lame leg is either inborn through some thwarting of the Reason-Principle, or is a marring of the achievement form by accident. To that Intellectual Kosmos belong qualities, accordant with nature . . . But there time is replaced by eternity and space by mutual inclusiveness'.[53]

The meaning is clear. The Intellectual-Principle is the idea of the universe—the ideal archetype. Of course I am speaking of the Intellectual-Principle as νοητά or Being. The concept is clearly Platonic, with this exception. According to Plato the ideas are essential universal thoughts, but because they are universal, they are not somebody's thoughts. They are thoughts apart from a thinker. Plotinus also regards them as essential universal thoughts, but because God is a universal concept, they are the thoughts of God. The Intellectual-Principle as νοῦς thinks itself as νοητά. Thinker and thought are therefore identical. There is therefore no danger that the ideas can be regarded as subjective, because they are the content of a universal concept. Nor can they be regarded as alien to the Intellectual Principle, because they are the νοητά, and the νοητά are merely logically distinguished from the νοῦς. Essentially they are one.

In many respects the νοητά are more satisfactory than the ideas of Plato. The Platonic ideas have no mutual unity. It is true that Plato speaks of a hierarchy, but he does not elaborate that hierarchy, and it would be impossible for anybody to do so. The fact that the idea 'Goodness' is placed at the top of the scale, is also unsatisfactory.

How can it include the idea of dirt? What is there in the idea of Goodness that makes it the supreme concept? Apart from these considerations we must remember that the idea of Goodness was, to Plato, thinkable. Like the other ideas, it had to be reached by human discursive reasoning. But if it were the unifying principle of the ideas, it would itself have been a unity, a simplex; and a simplex, as we have already pointed out, is not knowable by the discursive reasoning of man.

The νοητά of Plotinus, on the other hand, are distinguished from one another without ever losing their essential unity. They are one. Plato has an idea for every object. Plotinus in his νοητά has one cosmic idea. The utter transcendence of that cosmic idea is embodied in the One. It is itself a unity and a potential multiplicity. It is the One-in-many.

Plato tells us that even ugly and unnatural things have their ideal archetypes. It appears, therefore, that the ideas of Plato are little more than a mechanical replica of the universe. But Plotinus says: 'There is no question of an ideal archetype of evil: the evil of this world is begotten of need, privation, deficiency and is a condition peculiar to Matter distressed and to what has come into likeness with Matter'.[54]

It is clear that the Intellectual-Principle is a teleological concept. It is the universe as it exists in the mind of God, and because the thoughts of God must of necessity be translated into realities, the real universe of his thoughts is transplanted on Matter. The ideas are not a copy of the visible universe. The visible universe is an imperfect copy of the ideas. Plato could never give a satisfactory explanation of evil, but for Plotinus evil is simply a stage in the development of the creative vision of the Intellectual-Principle.

Plato's ideas are the universe as it is. The νοητά of Plotinus are the universe as it should be. It is the teleological goal of the visible universe, the vision in the heart of the artist who, it is true, succeeds in translating that vision on canvas or in music, but never perfectly. Plotinus sees in the visible universe a striving after God, just as St. Paul who speaks of the whole creation being in travail. It is the teleological principle of the universe, the plan according to which the development of the universe takes place. And that, too, is for Plotinus the *modus quo* of divine creation—an ever progressive approach of the temporal to the eternal. The modern theory of evolution would not have been strange for Plotinus. He would simply have regarded it as the orderly manifestation of eternal and universal principles in a space-time sphere, the realization of the cosmic idea in the visible universe.

It is, therefore, not strange that the νοητά of Plotinus are not a mechanical copy of the world as we know it.

'But on the question as to whether the repulsive and the products of putridity have also their idea—whether there is an idea of filth and mud—it is to be observed that all that the Intellectual-Principle derived from the First is of the noblest; in those ideas the base is not included: these repulsive things point not to the Intellectual-Principle but to the Soul which, drawing upon the Intellectual-Principle, takes from Matter certain things, and among them these . . . The products of putrefaction are to be traced to the Soul's inability to bring some other thing to being'.[55]

On the surface it may appear as if Plotinus regards the creative power as a dualism, but that is not the case. The fact that there are concepts in the visible world whose archetypes are not in the νοητά, does not mean that there is another creator, but merely that the creative νοητά experience the resistance of matter and that the image of the Intellectual-Principle can on that account not be perfectly realized in the world. In other words, the existence of evil does not point to an evil creator or that there are two opposite creating deities, but merely that the creation of the visible universe, or, to view the process from the other side, the realization of the image of God, is not a *fiat*, but a process of development, where resistance is not only possible but even unavoidable. There is no doubt that in this respect Plotinus is far in advance of Plato.

The νοητά of Plotinus do not, like the Platonic ideas, form a hierarchy. They are a unity. We should, in fact, speak of a κόσμος νοητός, an ideal universe or a cosmic idea, rather than of νοητά. There is, as we have seen, in the cosmic idea of Plotinus, merely the logical dualism of thinker and thought, that, and nothing more. And even then, there is in fact no dualism, because thinker and thought are one. Already in the visible universe Plotinus sees a unity which is diminished by the subjection to the special character of material things. But in the cosmic idea there is no such subjection. The universe is a vision of God. Its teleology is directed to one purpose. There is no separate striving by separate ideas to realize that of which it is the essence. The Cosmic Idea strives as a unity. There is one single plan.

> 'For I feel that through the ages,
> One increasing purpose runs'.

That increasing purpose is nothing else than the progressive realization of the Cosmic Idea in the material sphere. This fact will become clearer when later we deal with the *modus quo* of the creative activities in the system of Plotinus.

## The Intellectual-Principle as Nous

We have, so far, confined ourselves to the discussion of the Intellectual-Principle as content and object of thought. Up to this point we have found a parallel in Plato. His Ideas were thoughts, although not the thoughts of any thinker. With Plotinus it is otherwise. The νοητά, notwithstanding their unity, would have been absolutely separate from one another, had it not been for the fact that they are the thoughts of the Intellectual-Principle. To put the matter differently: the universe would have been a multiverse, an infinite number of copies of an infinite number of ideas, with no essential unity except the arbitrarily super-imposed Idea of the Good. With Plotinus the Cosmic Idea is the thought, or vision, of the Cosmic Teleology, the Intellectual-Principle.

'We repeat that the Intellectual-Principle must have, actually has, self-vision, firstly because it has multiplicity, next because it exists for the external and therefore must be a seeing power, one seeing that external. In fact, its very essence is vision; and if there be nothing external the Intellectual-Principle exists in vain'.

In other words, God and the creation presuppose one another. Unless there is thought, or as Plotinus has it, vision, in the Intellectual Principle, there can be no contact between the Ideal World and the visible universe. It is the essence of the Intellectual-Principle to have vision, and that vision is in fact the active principle of its teleology. It sees or thinks itself, and that vision is progressively realized in the material universe.

What, actually, is the seeing or thinking phase in the Intellectual-Principle, and what is the object of its vision? Plotinus says: 'Admiring the world of sense as we look out upon its vastness and beauty and the order of its eternal march, thinking of the gods within it, seen and hidden, and the celestial spirits and all the life of animal and plant, let us mount to its archetype, to the yet more authentic sphere: there we are to contemplate all things as members of the Intellectual—eternal in their own right, vested with a self-springing consciousness and life—and, presiding over all these, the unsoiled Intelligence and the unapproachable Wisdom . . . Here is contained all that is immortal: nothing here but a Divine Mind; all is God . . . Its knowing is not by search but by possession, its blessedness inherent, not acquired . . . Soul deals with thing after thing—now Socrates; now a horse: always some one entity from among beings—but the Intellectual-Principle is all and therefore its entire content is simultaneously present in that identity: This is pure Being in eternal actuality . . . And everything, in that entire content is Intellectual-Principle and Authentic Existence, and the total of all is Intellectual Principle entire and Being entire'.[56]

The meaning is clear. The seer or thinker in the Intellectual-Principle is identical with the νοητά or object of that vision. The Cosmic Idea is a thinking unity, a simplex, where the only duality is the logical dualism of agent and object of thought.

How does it think itself? As Plotinus says, it is pure Being in eternal actuality. Because its entire content is simultaneously and immediately present, its knowledge is not by search but by immediate possession. In other words, while our knowledge is acquired by discursive reasoning, by analysis and synthesis, the self-knowledge or self-vision of the Cosmic Idea is immediate. Plotinus points out that true self-knowledge can only belong to a simplex. When an entity consists of parts, where one part knows the other, we cannot correctly speak of self-knowledge. That would be merely knowledge of something external, but in the Intellectual-Principle νοῦς and νοητά are identical. When we know, we know by analysis and synthesis, but we always remain apart from the object of our knowledge. Such human thought and knowledge is based on poverty. We would not seek by discursive reasoning for something already our own. But in the Intellectual-Principle knower and known, seer and seen, are identical. The Cosmic Content is a unity, and therefore the vision or the knowledge is immediate. Plotinus asks: 'Has our discussion issued in an Intellectual-Principle having a discursive knowledge-seeking activity? No, it brings immediate knowledge, not discursive knowledge. Immediate knowledge belongs to the Intellectual-Principle, discursive knowledge to the soul or mind'.[57]

The knowledge of the Intellectual Principle is therefore self-knowledge, and it is immediate. The relation of νοῦς and νοητά, of Cosmic Thought and Cosmic Content, is one of identity. But nevertheless Plotinus is eager to point out that notwithstanding this identity there is duality and even multiplicity in the Intellectual-Principle. Had it been an absolute simplex, thought would have been impossible. We have already seen that the One is above thought, for this very reason.

Superficially it may appear as if Plotinus is here contradicting his own words. After stressing the unity of the Intellectual-Principle, he says: 'This principle knows immediately (πρώτως νοεῖ), since there can be no intellection without unity and duality. If there is no unity, perceiving principle and perceived object will be different, and the intellection, therefore, not immediate: a principle concerned with something external cannot have immediate knowledge since it does not possess the object as integrally its own or as itself; if it does possess the object as itself—the condition of true intellection—the two are one. Thus there must be a unity in duality, while a pure unity with no counterbalancing duality can have no object for its intellection and ceases to be intellective. In other words, the immediately-knowing entity must be at once a simplex and something else'.[58]

We have already seen, in our discussion of the question, whether multiplicity can emerge from the One, that a satisfactory answer to this question is essential. Here we have the most important aspect of Plotinus' answer. The Absolute is a One-in-Many. When applied to the Intellectual-Principle, we may say that it is the many because all the items in the universe can be referred to that Principle in its nature as Cosmic Idea; it is a unity because in it all those otherwise disjointed items find their common source and their unity. In a later chapter, when dealing with the Plotinian theory of the *modus quo* of creation, we shall see that this combination of multiplicity and unity in the Intellectual-Principle is an essential condition in its creative activity. The Intellectual-Principle sees itself. The vision is the νοητά, the Cosmic Idea, and because its vision, thought or contemplation, is dynamic, the visible universe comes into being. There must be unity, because the seeing aspect must be one. Because the visible universe is the product of the vision of a unity, there is unity of purpose in creation. The apparently disjointed items work towards one common goal, they are governed by one common law. And had it not been for the multiplicity, all would have remained barren. A visible universe where there is a unity of purpose and a multiplicity of items could not have been the product of the vision of a Principle where there is merely unity, while on the other hand, a universe without the multiplicity of items is unthinkable.

This is in fact nothing more than the Platonic system of ideas with essential unity super-imposed. I say essential, because the Platonic ideas have no essential unity. The so-called hierarchy is not essential. Plato's system gives no explanation of the common law and the common purpose. At most, it postulates the existence of an ideal world, but an ideal world consisting of disjointed ideas, of which the visible universe is no counterpart, because it is a counterpart of the visible world. We may as well believe in the water-babies of Charles Kingsley, as in the ideas of Plato. There are water-rats and land-rats, water-flies and land-flies, water-crabs and land-crabs. So why not water-babies and land-babies? Plato would say: There are particular horses, particular colours, particular cases of nonsense. So why not a universal horse, a universal colour, a universal nonsense?

## The Categories of the Intellectual-Principle

Although it is really in the sixth *Ennead* that Plotinus deals at length with the categories, we find a clear synopsis in *Enn*. v. 1, 4, where he says: 'Thus the Primals [τὰ πρῶτα] are Nous [νοῦς], Being [ὄν], Difference [ἑτερότης], Sameness [ταυτότης]. We must include also Motion [κίνησις] and Rest [στάσις]. Motion provides for the intellectual act, rest preserves the identity. We postulate difference, so that there may be thought and object of thought'. In *Ennead* vi. 2, 15 he omits Nous and Being. 'Being', he says, 'is primary and it is clear that none of the four—Motion, Stability, Difference, Identity—are distinct from it'. In vi. 2, 8 he postulates five categories, leaving out Nous.

It were futile to follow Plotinus in his long and weary discussion of the categories in general. What he means by categories is given in *Ennead* vi. 2, 4, where he says: 'If we had to ascertain the nature of body and the place it holds in the universe, surely we should take some sample of body, say stone, and examine into what constituents it may be divided. There would be what we think of as the sub-stratum of stone, its quantity—in this case, a magnitude, its quality—

for example, the colour of stone. As with stone, so with every other body, there are three distinguishable characteristics—the pseudo-substance, the quantity, the quality—though they all make one and are only logically trisected, the three being found to constitute the unit thing, body. If motion were equally inherent in its constitution, we should include this as well, and the four would form a unity, the single body depending upon them all for its unity and characteristic nature'.[59]

But, Plotinus proceeds, in the case of the Intellectual-Principle we must abstract all the characteristics of a corporeal entity, that is to say, all those characteristics which produce isolation and mutual separation. 'It is an Intellectual Being we have to consider, an Authentic Existent, possessed of a unity surpassing that of any sensible thing'.[60]

Plotinus sees the crux of the matter in the question how a unity of this type can at the same time be a many, and he finds his answer in the sensible objects of the visible world. Their multiplicity is in every case—individually and collectively—bound by unity. 'Bodies . . . are each a multiplicity, founded on colour and shape and magnitude, and on the form and arrangement of parts: yet all these elements spring from a unity'.[61] In the same way the multiplicity of objects, the multiversal nature of the visible world, has a unity superimposed. That unity is of course the common goal, the common law governing the universe, the 'one increasing purpose', of which he says that it is higher than the unity found in any particular object, but lower than the unity found in the Cosmic Idea. He calls the unity of the visible world a pluralized unity [$εἶναι ἐκ πλήθους ἑνός$[62]] which, as we shall see later, is the third hypostasis of the Ultimate Reality, Soul, the immanent phase of the Godhead. That Soul is the creative $λόγος$ of the Intellectual-Principle, the creator of particular entities, from which the universe derives its pluralized unity. Soul must therefore be itself a unity-in-plurality.

But Soul is a Reason-Principle, a Logos,[63] one with the Intellectual-Principle. Therefore the Intellectual-Principle is also a One-in-Many [$πλῆθος ἕν$].

This, then, is the basis of the Plotinian categories of the Intellectual-Principle, a non-corporeal pluralized unity.

Let us now take these categories singly. In the first place, there is life in the Intellectual Being. Movement is a category common to all life. Motion is therefore a category of the Intellectual-Principle.

But, he says, motion so manifested in conjunction with Being, does not alter Being's nature, because there is also Stability, in other words 'unalterable condition, unchanging mode, single Logos— these are characteristics of the higher sphere. [τὸ γὰρ κατὰ ταὐτὰ καὶ ὡσαύτως καὶ ἕνα λόγον ἔχον, ἐκεῖ.⁶⁴]. Plotinus points out that, although Motion and Stability are essential categories of Being, they are nevertheless not to be identified with it. 'To identify Stability with Being, with no difference between them, and to identify Being with Motion, would be to identify Stability with Motion through the mediation of Being, and so to make Motion and Stability one and the same thing'.⁶⁵

We have, then, Being, Motion and Stability, three *genera* which are free of matter and are purely *genera* of the Intellectual World. But with Being [τὸ ὄν] we must postulate thought. 'In virtue of its Being it thinks, and it thinks itself as Being'.⁶⁶

These three categories of Being, Motion and Stability, with Thought added, as a necessary correlative to Being, show that there is a clear distinction in the categories of the Intellectual-Principle, but no separation. They are logical postulates of that Principle 'an all-embracing unity'.⁶⁷ There is therefore difference and identity.

So Plotinus postulates these categories also, namely Identity and Difference. Here we have six categories, while in *Ennead* v. 1, 4, as we have seen, he postulates only five, leaving out Thought or Nous. But as we shall see, Nous is a necessary correlative to Being.

The similarity between the categories of Plato and Plotinus is patent. Plato postulates Being and Non-Being [τὸ μὴ εἶναι], Identity and Difference, Permanence and Change. The last two are merely synonyms for Stability and Movement. The categories of Being and Non-Being are of course related to the Platonic theory that absolute Being is the absolutely knowable, and absolute Non-Being absolutely unknowable,⁶⁸ and therefore points to the intellectually transcendent and knowable aspects of Ultimate Reality.

As Inge points out,⁶⁹ the Platonic categories tend to supersede the ideas in the later dialogues, and my own criticism points the same way. I have no quarrel with the Platonic categories. My difficulty is that I fail to see how the Platonic categories have anything in common with the Platonic ideas. Being, Difference and Permanence I can understand. Being, because the Platonic ideas are knowable. They are concepts open to the discursive reasoning of man; Differ-

ence, because they are a multiplicity; Permanence, because there is
no thought, no movement, no thinker. But what of Non-Being?
If Non-Being means the absolutely unknowable, where do we find
in Plato any indication that his world of ideas transcends knowledge? Is that world of ideas an unknowable simplex? Why, even
the supreme idea of the Good is a concept open to man. What of
identity? What is the unifying principle in the Platonic ideas?
The supposed hierarchy? Is that hierarchy essential, or is it arbitrarily postulated? What logical necessity is there why the idea of
dirt should be included in and encompassed by the supreme idea of
the Good? And what of Change? There are the eternal, universal
ideas. That is Permanence. In the same way Plotinus postulates
Stability, or the νοητά. But what movement is there in the Platonic
ideas? Is there dynamic contemplation or thought or vision whereby
the universal is reflected in the particular? Surely it cannot be that
illegal immigrant, the Demiurgos, of whom Plato speaks in his
*Timaios*?

With Plotinus it is different. His categories correspond to the rest
of his system. They are the necessary characteristics of an ultimate
Reality that is a One-in-many. There are three pairs of categories
in Plotinus, and it is easy to see that they form, in reality, two
correlatives. Being, Stability, and Identity are the correlatives of
Thought, Movement, and Difference. Being is identified with the
νοητά, Thought with the νοῦς. That νοῦς is also Movement.

That was the old problem—to reconcile the continual change of
the universe with the concept of a higher stability, superseding all
the change, unifying all the diversity. Parmenides was probably
the first thinker who became aware of the problem, but in his
attempts to find the eternal in the changing world, he wrongly
robbed Being of all movement and change. He could find no
contact between Being and the world of change. Heraclitus touched
the other extreme, with the result that he missed the governing idea
of unity in the universe.

Perhaps the one who, before Plotinus, most nearly reached the
solution of the problem, was Anaxagoras, who found in his Nous
the immovable basis of movement. But, like Plato, he failed to
explain how Nous was the cause of that movement.

But before Plotinus no thinker realized that the Absolute must
in truth be a unity, but that an abstract monism would fail to serve
as an explanation of the existence of the visible universe. Had God

been a barren unity without multiplicity or movement, He would not have been the *causa efficax* of the world.

The opposite is also true. Had God been merely multiplicity, we would have been at a loss to explain the unity of the universe. The innumerable disjointed items would have exhibited no unity. The Whole needs a single author before the multiverse can be a universe. That was the work of Plotinus. Movement and Stability are both essential categories of his Intellectual-Principle. God is a One-in-many. Movement and Stability find their counterparts in Nous and νοητά respectively—in Thought, Movement, in Being, Stability.

In the categories, Difference and Identity, we have the same distinction. Superficially the universe exhibits a disjointed collection of incoherent entities. But our thought demands a transcendent unity to form the basis of the multiplicity. The basic standpoint of Plotinus and of all Idealism is that the mutual relationship of things is to be found in the immanence of the temporal in the eternal. The 'little flower in the crannied wall' holds within it the secret of all human and divine history. 'The Whole is present and active within everything—is immanent, if we desire a technical term; conversely, everything, at bottom and in its full nature, implies the Whole, and can never be truly comprehended except as it takes its place and fulfils its function within the Whole'.⁷⁰

And if we seek this reconciliation even in the visible universe, all the more are we entitled to find it in the Intellectual-Principle, because that Principle is the Cosmic Idea, the archetype of the visible cosmos.

Our only criticism of the categories of Plotinus would be that there are in reality only two, and not six categories; Being, Stability, Identity are actually one, the Absolute which is eternally itself. Thought, Movement and Difference are the Absolute in its character of the Nous, the dynamic creator through whose vision the stable νοητά become the logical archetype of the visible universe.

The categories of Plotinus are the expression of his superiority over Greek thinkers before his time. What the Christian regards as a mystery to be approached only in humble worship, that God is three persons and one substance, was to Plotinus the necessary postulate of logical thought. It is no supernatural wonder that God is a One-in-Many. It would have been incomprehensible had He been anything else.

## The Intellectual-Principle and the Universe

The relation of the Platonic ideas to the visible universe is one of the questions which Plato was unable to answer. He tells us that particular entities, 'participate' in the ideas, that they are copies of those ideas. But apparently Plato himself found this answer unsatisfactory, and in the *Timaios* he produces a god to form the link between the universal and the particular. The *Timaios* is in fact the expression of the insolvency of Platonic metaphysics. The production of a *tertium quid* to form the link is a confession that there is in fact no link. Aristotle's criticism of Plato was perhaps in some respects unfair, but I think he was right in regarding this matter as the main weakness in the Platonic system.

It is in this respect that Plotinus shows his superiority. It is not my intention at this stage to discuss in detail the *modus quo* of Neo-Platonic creation. That is a matter to be dealt with under the third hypostasis of the Plotinian Godhead. Broadly speaking, we could say that the universe is the product of the self-vision of the Intellectual-Principle, the realization of the νοητά as the object of the vision of the Nous. 'We repeat that the Intellectual-Principle must have, actually has, self-vision, firstly because it has multiplicity, next because it exists for the external and therefore must be a seeing power, one seeing that external; in fact, its very essence is vision. Given some external, there must be vision; and if there be nothing external, the Intellectual-Principle exists in vain. Unless there be something beyond bare unity, there can be no vision; vision must converge with a visible object. And this which the seer is to see can be only a multiple, no undistinguishable unity; nor could a universal unity find anything upon which to exercise any act; all, one and desolate, would be utter stagnation; in so far as there is action, there is diversity. If there be no distinctions, what is there to do, what direction in which to move? An agent must either act upon the extern or be a multiple and so act upon itself; making no advance towards anything other than itself, it is motionless and where it could know only blank fixity, it can know nothing. The intellective power, when occupied with the intellectual act, must be in a state of duality, whether one of the two elements stand actually outside or both lie within; the intellectual act will always comport diversity as well as the necessary identity, and in the same way its characteristic objects must stand to the Intellectual-Principle at once distant and identical. This applies equally to the single object; there can be no intellection except of something containing separable detail and, since the object is a Logos, it has the necessary element of multiplicity. The Intellectual-Principle thus, is informed of itself by the fact of being a multiple organ of vision, an eye receptive of many illuminated objects. If it had to direct itself to a member-less unity, it would be dereasoned: what could it say or know of such an object? The self-affirmation of a memberless unity implies the repudiation of all that does not enter into the character. In other words, it must be multiple as a preliminary to being itself. Then again, in the assertion 'I am this particular thing', either the 'particular' thing is distinct from the assertor—and there is a false statement—or it is included within it, and, at once, multiplicity is asserted: otherwise the assertion is 'I am what I am' or 'I am I'. If it be no more than a simple duality to say 'I and that other phase', there is already multiplicity, for there is distinction and ground for distinction, there is number with all its train of separate things. In sum, then, a knowing principle must handle distinct items: its object must, at the moment of cognition, contain diversity: otherwise the thing remains unknown; there is mere conjunction, such a contact, without affirmation or comprehension, as would precede knowledge, the intellect not yet in being, the impinging agent not the percipient. Similarly the knowing principle cannot remain simplex, especially in the act of self knowing: all silent though its self-perception be, it is dual to itself'.[71]

The most important statement in this passage is that the Intellectual-Principle exists for something external. By virtue of its self-vision it is a duality, and by virtue of that duality there is a relation between it and the universe.

Plotinus makes much of the truth that the Intellectual-Principle cannot be a barren unity. Nevertheless, he says that 'the characteristic objects of its vision [and by that he means the ideas] stand to the Intellectual-Principle as at once distinct and identical'. In other words, the different aspects are logically distinguished but actually identical. Can it then be anything else but a unity? It can, by virtue of the fact that although those aspects are actually identical, they are nevertheless aspects and therefore distinguished from one another, although not separate. Thought presupposes duality because thought demands a knowable entity within or without the knower. If without, then that knower is multiple because it stands in relation

D

to something external; if within, there is none the less multiplicity, because a simplex cannot be the object of knowledge.

But we must guard against the supposition that the one aspect of the Intellectual-Principle knows the other aspect, while itself remains unknown. The νοῦς is the νοητά, or rather, both are the Intellectual-Principle, but the one as Intellectual-Principle knowing, the other as Intellectual-Principle known. In the cited passage Plotinus says that 'its characteristic objects must stand to the Intellectual-Principle as at once distinct and identical'. Had the knowing aspect known a separate known aspect, the known aspect would have remained ignorant and the knowing aspect unknown. And even had this knowledge been mutual, there would have been distinct parts. The Intellectual-Principle is a unity in everything except in the fact that it thinks. 'Does it all come down, then, to one phase of the self knowing the other phase? That would be a case of knower distinguished from known, and could not be self-knowing . . . The object known must be identical with the knowing act, the Intellectual-Principle, therefore, identical with the Intellectual Realm'.[72]

We must, however, not be misled by the word 'thought' or 'knowledge' used here. The thought, vision or knowledge of the Intellectual-Principle is immediate. It does not follow the discursive road of analysis and synthesis.

But what, then, is the external of which we read in the cited passage and which serves as the object of the vision of the Intellectual-Principle? Are there, then, two objects of that vision, one the Intellectual-Principle itself and the other the external universe? And if that is the case, what becomes of the vaunted self-identity of knower and known in the Intellectual-Principle?

The answer to this question we find in the rather difficult tractate on *Contemplation*, where Plotinus states that contemplation and action are two grades of the same activity. When we 'see' something we must have recourse to action before our vision becomes actuality. But the vision of the Intellectual-Principle is dynamic. It becomes actuality without action. 'And Nature, asked why it brings forth its works, might answer if it cared to listen and to speak: . . . Whatsoever comes into being is my vision, seen in my silence, the vision that belongs to my character who, sprung from vision, am vision-loving and create vision by the vision-seeing faculty within me. The mathematicians from their vision draw their figures: but I draw nothing. I gaze, and the figures of the material world take being as if they fall from my contemplation. As with my Mother (Plotinus here means the Universal Soul) and the Beings that begot me, so it is with me: they are born of a contemplation, and my birth is from them, not by their Act but by their Being, they are the loftier Logoi. They contemplate themselves and I am born'.[73]

The self-vision of the Intellectual-Principle can therefore not be barren. It becomes the involuntary and unconscious 'fiat' of divine creation. The Nous sees the νοητά, and the universe, or reflection of the νοητά, comes into being. The Intellectual-Principle therefore exists for the visible universe not in the sense that it sees that universe or is even conscious of it. Plotinus clearly states that the Intellectual-Principle has only self-vision. And yet it knows the visible universe more completely than we know that universe, because the objects of its knowledge are the νοητά, and the νοητά are the Cosmic Idea, the Universal Universe of which the universe as we know it is merely the reflection, the imperfect copy, just as the Platonic ideas are the archetypes of the things here below.

And yet with a difference. Our universe is not a mechanical replica of the νοητά. As we shall see later in our treatment of evil, the vile and the evil things on earth have no archetype in the Ideal world. Those things are merely the result of the multiplicity-in-actuality caused by the material substratum of our universe. The νοητά are therefore the ideal also in the sense that in the Ideal world, in the Cosmic Idea, we have the measure of perfection in the visible world. It is the teleological aspect of the Ideal world, the divine plan of the universe, the manifested God, whose manifestation is the universe.

Consequently, according to Plotinus, the visible universe has no more than a derived reality. It is real only in so far as it approaches the Cosmic Idea. In our discussion in a later chapter of the visible universe we will see that visible entities consist of two aspects—the material and the formal. The material aspect is negative. It is the τὸ μὴ ὄν, the negation of reality, not merely its absence. Only the formal, with its archetype in the Cosmic Idea, is in a measure real. From this I derive the theory which I believe I see in Plotinus, that the Intellectual-Principle is the basis of our scale of values. I shall discuss this theory in terms of the three values of truth, beauty and goodness.

That Plotinus regarded the Intellectual-Principle as the basis of truth is certain. As Idealist he could, in the midst of change and mutual contradictions, have sought in the Universal a criterion for truth. That was the excellence of Plato, that he represents the antithesis to the subjectivism of the Sophists with their practical negation of objective truth, and that he found in the universal ideas the metaphysical basis of truth. But the ideas of Plato lacked unity. Each entity in the particular universe would then have had its criterion in the universal idea, but because those ideas were nothing more than a mechanical universalization of the particular, there was no absolute metaphysical basis for truth. A horse would, it is true, have been real in so far as it participated in the idea 'horse', and so with other things, but actually it means little more than that there was a definite definition for every entity and that such definition gave the essential characteristics of such an entity. To put the matter differently, the visible universe is in that case not really a copy of the ideal world, but the ideal world is postulated on the basis of what the philosopher sees in the visible world. His criterion of truth was therefore based on the appearance of those entities to which it had to serve as a criterion. There is no teleology, and without that no basis of truth can satisfy the demands of logic.

With Plotinus it is otherwise. The νοητά are no glorified spiritualization of the total of visible and particular entities. There is teleology. Something is true not in the measure of its participation in the universal idea of that particular thing, but in the measure of its approach to or participation in the Cosmic Idea. 'Our reasoning is our own; we ourselves think the thoughts that occupy the understanding, . . . but the operation of the Intellectual-Principle enters from above us as that of the sensitive faculty from below . . . The sensitive principle is our scout; the Intellectual-Principle is our king. But we, too, are king when we are moulded to the Intellectual-Principle. That correspondence may be brought about in two ways: either the radii from that centre are traced upon us to be our law or we are filled full of Divine Mind'.[74]

The clear meaning of Plotinus in this passage becomes still clearer in the next citation where he postulates the existence of truth on the basis of correspondence between νοῦς and νοητά in the Intellectual-Principle.

'In order to perfect self-knowing it must bring over from itself the knowing phase as well: seeing subject and seen objects must be present as one thing. Now if in this coalescence of seeing subject with seen objects, the objects were merely representations of the reality, the subject would not possess the realities; if it does possess them it must do so not by seeing them as the result of any self-division, but by knowing them, containing them, before any self-division occurs. At that, the object known must be identical with the knowing act, the Intellectual-Principle, therefore, identical with the Intellectual Realm. And in fact, if this identity does not exist, neither does truth; the Principle that should contain realities is found to contain a transcript, something different from the realities; that constitutes non-Truth. Truth cannot apply to something conflicting with itself; what it affirms it must also be'.[75]

Inge[76] affirms, wrongly, that truth for Plotinus is the correspondence of thought with object. It is in fact the identity of thought and object, and this identity is found only in the Intellectual-Principle. Truth is possible only in the universe where Nous and *νοητά* are one.

That Plotinus also regarded the Intellectual-Principle as criterion of beauty, is easier to prove, because he devotes a separate tractate[77] to the treatment of this problem. In a later chapter on Aesthetics we will discuss the matter in greater detail, but at this stage the following passage from the *Enneads* will suffice.

'Thus there is in the Nature-Principle an Ideal archetype of the beauty [λόγος κάλλους ἀρχέτυπος] that is found in material forms, and of that archetype again, the still more beautiful archetype in Soul, source of that in Nature. In the proficient Soul [ἐν σπουδαία ψυχῇ, i.e. the human soul that is in contact with the Universal World, or God], this is brighter and of more advanced loveliness; adorning the soul and bringing to it a light from that greater light which is beauty primally [ἀπὸ φωτὸς μείζονος πρώτως κάλλους ὄντος] . . . This prior, then, is the Intellectual-Principle'.[78]

In the same way the Intellectual-Principle is the source of our goodness. We must, however, be careful not to confuse this concept with the epithet 'Good' as applied to the One. That epithet, as we know, is not given as a positive attribute. The One transcends goodness, and any name given to it is given only because 'we do not know what else to call it'.

According to Plotinus any moral judgment that we pass is of value only because we possess inherently the Intellectual-Principle. In other words, only because we have our archetype in the Cosmic Idea, we can distinguish between good and evil. 'Sense sees a man and transmits the impression to the understanding. What does the understanding say? It has nothing to say as yet; it accepts and waits; unless, rather, it questions within itself: 'Who is this?'—someone it has met before—and then, drawing on memory, says, 'Socrates'. If it should go on to develop the impression received, it distinguishes various elements in what the representative faculty has set before it; supposing it to say: 'Socrates, if the man is good', then, while it has spoken upon information from the senses, its total pronouncement is its own; it contains within itself a standard of good. But how does it thus contain the good within itself? It is, itself, of the nature of the good and it has been strengthened still towards the perception of all that is good by the irradiation of the Intellectual-Principle upon it; for this pure phase of the soul welcomes to itself the images implanted from its prior [i.e. the Intellectual-Principle'.][79]

I have touched on these problems only superficially. In our treatment of the Epistemology, Ethics and Aesthetics of Plotinus the question will be dealt with in greater detail. But as a preliminary conclusion we may say that the metaphysical basis of moral obligation, of beauty and truth, is to be found in the Intellectual-Principle. That Principle is a teleological concept—the archetype of the visible universe. 'Consider the universe; we are agreed that its existence and its nature come to it from beyond itself; are we, now, to imagine that its maker first thought it out in detail—the earth, and its necessary situation in the middle; water and, again, its position as lying upon the earth; all the other elements and objects up to the sky in due order; living beings with their appropriate forms as we know them, their inner organs and their outer limits—and that having thus appointed every item beforehand, he then set about the execution? Such designing was not even possible; how could the plan for a universe come to one that had never looked outward? . . . One way only remains: all things must exist in something else; of that prior . . . there has suddenly appeared a sign, an image, whether given forth directly or through the ministry of soul or some phase of soul, matters nothing for the moment; thus the entire aggregate of existence springs from the divine world, in greater beauty There because There unmingled but mingled here . . . The exemplar was the Idea of an All and so an All must come into being'.[80]

Have we, in the light of these considerations, the right to consider the Intellectual-Principle as the God of Neo-Platonism? In the first place it must be pointed out that the Intellectual-Principle is not an absolute unity and consequently we are constrained to seek above that Principle for a comprehensive unity. And in respect of the relation between the Intellectual-Principle and the universe there are a number of *lacunae* where a further link is necessary. There is, for instance, the question of its immanence. Plotinus apparently recognized the immanence of the Intellectual-Principle in certain entities, e.g. in man, but then always as a dormant potentiality which need not be brought to actuality. 'Again there must be something prior to Soul because Soul is in the world and there must be something outside a world in which, all being corporeal and material, nothing has enduring reality: failing such a prior, neither man nor the Ideas would be eternal or have true identity'.[81]

In this passage the transcendence of the Intellectual-Principle is clearly postulated against the immanence of the Soul. The opposite view seems to be given in the next citation. 'All that one sees as a spectacle is still external; one must bring the vision within and see no longer in that mode of separation but as we know ourselves; thus a man filled with a God need no longer look outside for his vision of the divine being; it is but finding the strength to see divinity within'.[82]

The conciliation of these two apparently opposite views lies in the thought that the universe, as image of the Intellectual-Principle, must participate in that Principle, but not everywhere in the same measure. There is no possibility that we, as human beings, can have the cosmic idea as object of our thoughts and knowledge, because that would make the Intellectual-Principle a multiplicity instead of merely a logical multiplicity and actual unity. We can know the Cosmic Idea only partially by knowing that entity which participates in the Cosmic Idea in the largest measure, and that entity is man. The Intellectual-Principle as involuntary author of the universe must transcend the universe, and by virtue of that transcendence the universe participates or is immanent in that Principle.

This view is very clearly stated in the following passages. 'All, then, that is present in the sense-realm as Idea, comes from the Supreme. But what is not present as Idea, does not. Thus of things conflicting with nature, none is There . . . There is no question of an Ideal archetype of evil: the evil of this world is begotten of need, privation, deficiency and is a condition peculiar to Matter distressed and to what has come into likeness with Matter'.[83] The second passage is even more explicit. 'Similarly any one, unable to see himself, but possessed by that God, has but to bring that divine-within before his consciousness and at once he sees an image of himself, himself lifted to a better beauty; now let him ignore that image, lovely though it is, and sink into a perfect self-identity, no such separation remaining; at once he forms a multiple unity with the God silently present'.[84]

In a certain sense, then, we can say that the Intellectual-Principle is immanent in the visible universe, but not in such a measure that our postulate for an immanent deity would thereby be satisfied. Nowhere does Plotinus say that the Intellectual-Principle is discreetly immanent in the various entities in the visible universe, and that we must come to the conclusion that the Intellectual-Principle alone cannot be called the God of Neo-Platonism. There must be a prior and a subsequent to satisfy our demand for transcendence absolute and immanence absolute. By itself it is nothing more than the teleological archetype, the Cosmic Idea, the 'one increasing purpose'. That prior we have already found in the One. It remains for us to find the subsequent, the Immanence Absolute. But before doing so, we shall have to examine more closely the relation of the Intellectual-Principle to its prior, the One.

### The Relation of the Intellectual-Principle to the One

We must now resume the arguments which were left in abeyance at the end of our discussion of the One. There we concluded that the One could not be regarded as a separate entity, and that such a supposition would not only be in conflict with the unequivocal statements of Plotinus himself, but that, even if it had been so, nobody would have succeeded in absolving the philosopher from the charge that his philosophy constitutes a hopeless dualism between the Absolute and the Particular. We shall now discuss this problem in more detail with reference to the relation between the Intellectual-Principle and the One.

Apparently we have here two graded concepts. A superficial study of the following passage would seem to raise the issue above all doubt.

'But how and what does the Intellectual-Principle see and, especially, how has it sprung from that which is to become the object of its vision? The mind demands the existence of these

Beings, but it is still in trouble over the problem endlessly debated by the most ancient philosophers: from such a unity as we have declared the One to be, how does anything at all come into substantial existence, any multiplicity, dyad or number? Why has the Primal not remained self-gathered so that there be none of this profusion of the manifold which we observe in existence and yet are compelled to trace to that absolute unity? . . . How the Divine Mind comes into being must be explained: Everything moving has necessarily an object towards which it moves. But since the Supreme can have no such object towards which it advances, we may not ascribe motion to it. Anything that comes into being after it, can be produced only as a consequence of its unfailing self-intention; and, of course, we dare not talk of generation in time, dealing as we are with eternal Beings; where we speak of origin in such reference, it is in the sense, merely, of cause and subordination; origin from the Supreme must not be taken to imply any movement in it; that would make the Being resulting from the movement not a second hypostasis but a third: the Movement would be the second hypostasis. Given this immobility in the Supreme, it can neither have yielded assent nor uttered decree nor stirred in any way towards the existence of a secondary. What happened then? . . . All that is fully achieved, engenders; therefore the eternally achieved engenders eternally an eternal being. At the same time, the offspring is always a minor. What, then, are we to think of the All-Perfect, but that it can produce nothing less than the very greatest that is later than itself. This greatest, later than the divine unity, must be the Divine Mind, and it must be the second of all existence, for it is that which sees the One on which alone it leans, while the First has no need whatever of it. The offspring of the prior to Divine Mind can be no other than that Mind itself and thus is the loftiest being in the universe, all else following upon it, the Soul, for example, being an utterance, an act of the Intellectual-Principle as that is an utterance an act of the One. That Principle looks to the First without mediation . . .'[85]

Superficially it would seem that this passage very clearly indicates a gradation between the One and the Intellectual-Principle and that is in fact the current opinion. Every commentator on Plotinus will tell us that his divinity is a graded Triad.

That was also my view until I studied in detail the relation of the Intellectual-Principle to the Soul, the third hypostasis of the Plotinian Godhead. The conclusion I reached there sent me back to the first problem, the relation of the One to the Intellectual-Principle, and although the explicit verdicts of Plotinus are not so frequent and so unequivocal in this case as in the case of the Intellectual-Principle and the Soul, it is nevertheless my view that there is enough such evidence together with the overwhelming weight of the evidence of logical deductions from verdicts of Plotinus, to decide the question in a way not at all in agreement with the current view of a graded Triad.

We must be reminded in the first place that Plotinus regards the One as exalted above thought or vision, while self-vision or immediate (i.e. non-discursive) self-thought is the essence of the Intellectual-Principle. These facts we have already proved in our previous discussions.

With these two facts I shall now compare the next citation from Plotinus, and at this stage I may say that this passage is by no means the only example one could find in the *Enneads*.

'For the Intellectual-Principle, by very definition, cannot be outside of itself; self-gathered and unalloyed, it is Intellectual-Principle through all the range of its being, and thus it possesses of necessity self-knowing, as a being immanent to itself and one having for function and essence to be purely and solely Intellectual-Principle. This is no doer; the doer, not self-intent but looking outward, will have knowledge, in some kind, of the external, but, if wholly of this practical order, need have no self-knowledge; where, on the contrary, there is no action—and of course the pure Intellectual-Principle cannot be straining after any absent good—the intention can be only towards the self; at once self-knowing becomes not only plausible but inevitable; what else could living signify in a being immune from action and existing in Intellect? The contemplating of God, we might answer. But to admit its knowing God is to be compelled to admit its self-knowledge. It will know what it holds from God, what God has given forth or may. Knowing God and His power, then, it knows itself, since it comes from Him'.[86]

There is no doubt whatsoever that the God of whom he speaks here, is the One. 'It comes from Him', Plotinus says, and he has already told us that the Intellectual-Principle comes from the One.

We are therefore entitled, on the strength of this passage, to say that:

1. The Intellectual Principle knows and contemplates only itself and nothing else. Its own content is the limit of its contemplation. That is its essence.

2. It is the essence of the Intellectual-Principle to contemplate the One. Knowledge of the One is for the Intellectual-Principle perfect self-knowledge.

The conclusion which we are entitled to make from these facts belong to the province of elementary logic. The One and the Intellectual-Principle are actually identical, even though they may be logically distinguished.

A more thorough study of the first passage cited in this chapter (v. 1, 6) reveals the same facts. 'How is it to spring from that which is to become the object of its vision? . . . The Divine Mind is that which sees the One on which alone it leans . . . That Principle looks to the First without meditation'. These three concepts taken at random from the quoted passage are surely conclusive. The One is the immediate object of the vision of the Intellectual-Principle. But in our treatment of the One we have heard repeatedly that the Intellectual-Principle is its own object of vision.

There are various other passages in Plotinus which teach us the same lesson. 'We may conclude that in the Intellectual-Principle itself there is complete identity of knower and known . . . by the fact that there, no distinction exists between Being and Knowing . . .'[87] 'It is a principle with us that one who has attained to the vision of the Intellectual Beauty and grasped the beauty of the Authentic Intellect will be able also to come to understand the Father and Transcendent of that Divine Being'.[88]

A further indication pointing to the same conclusion is that Plotinus often names the One equally with the Intellectual-Principle as involuntary authors of the universe. Both are absolutely free of all relation to *externa*. And finally, by way of direct evidence, Plotinus tells us that in the Ideal World, which must include the One, the Intellectual-Principle and the Soul, there is absolute unity. 'That is why in the Over-World each entity is all, while here, below, the single entity is not all [τὸ μὲν γὰρ ἄνω πᾶν πάντα τὰ δὲ κάτω οὐ πάντα ἕκαστον].[89]

We have already, in our discussion of the One, described it as the transcendent aspect of the Plotinian Godhead, and that, ultimately, is the explanation also given by Plotinus. It is the Unity-Principle of the Ideal World, and as such it cannot be separated from that Ideal World, the Cosmic Idea, which is the Intellectual-Principle. Every entity, Plotinus tells us, has such a principle, and nowhere can that principle be separated from the entity.

'Now when we reach a One—the abiding principle—in the tree, in the animal, in the soul, in the universe—we have in every case the most powerful, the precious element; when we come to the One in the Authentically Existent Beings—their Principle and source and potentiality—shall we lose confidence and suspect it of being nothing?'[90]

Our standpoint is that the One represents the transcendent Unity of God, the Intellectual-Principle its teleological nature. Neither concept can stand alone, and together they need a third concept to serve as a link with the universe. That link we shall find in the Soul.

# III

# THE SOUL

The Intellectual-Principle exhibits no satisfactory contact with the visible universe. Our logic demands some immanent concept to bridge the gulf between the Absolute and the Particular, and this concept we find in the Soul, or ψυχή, of Plotinus.

A few words should be said in connection with the name *Soul*. That is the usual word used by commentators of Plotinus to translate the concept ψυχή, and for that reason I have adopted it. But the translation is by no means satisfactory. The word ψυχή in Plotinus has different connotations of which only one, to a certain extent, approaches the meaning which we apply to our word *soul*.

In the first place there is Psyche as the third hypostasis of the Plotinian Godhead. For the sake of uniformity I call it Soul. A better translation would be Principle of Life. The second Psyche in the *Enneads* is the so-called World Soul of Plotinus, which commentators have wrongly confused with the third hypostasis of the Godhead. I have attempted to distinguish between the two concepts by rendering the latter Psyche by World-Soul. The third Psyche in Plotinus is something approaching our concept soul, or perhaps better, life. Plotinus distinguishes in this concept three phases or gradations which are not all necessarily present in the same entity. The lowest phase is the principle of growth which is found in all living things. In fact, not only does he see this vegetative phase of life in man, animals and plants, but because Plotinus does not accept any clear line of demarcation between animate and inanimate entities, he finds this vegetative phase of soul or life in most things. The second phase of the third Plotinian Psyche is the discursive reason which is the essentially human trait. The third and highest phase is the super-human aspect which is found in man only, but is not necessarily active in all men.[91] It is the organ by which we know God, and more will be said of it when we deal with the mysticism and religious aspects of the Plotinian system.

In this chapter we will restrict our discussion to Soul, or the Principle of Life, the third hypostasis of the Plotinian Godhead.

## The Origin of the Soul

If we regard the Soul as a separate entity which originated in the Intellectual-Principle, we meet with the same difficulties as in the case of the relation between that Principle and the One.

We know that the essence of the Intellectual-Principle is self-vision. The product of that self-vision is the visible universe; logically there is no room for a third entity, just as there was no logical possibility for the emanation of the Intellectual-Principle from the One.

The *modus quo* of the origin of the Soul is explained by Plotinus as an emanation from the essence of the Intellectual-Principle, of which it becomes the active power, the Logos.

'The second outflow is a Form or Idea representing the Divine Intellect as the Divine Intellect represented its own prior, the One. This active power sprung from Being [οὐσία, i.e. the Intellectual-Principle as νοητά] is Soul. Soul arises as the idea and act of the motionless Intellectual-Principle'.[92]

In our treatment of the categories of the Intellectual-Principle we have seen that Thought, Motion and Difference stand correlative to Being, Stability and Identity respectively. Thought is the Intellectual-Principle as νοῦς, Being as νοητά, the Cosmic Idea, the Ideal Universe. Soul is therefore the Logos, the creative Principle, of the Cosmic Idea. It fulfils the same function in the Plotinian system as the Demiurgos in the system of Plato.

In the same tractate Plotinus indicates that perfection generates towards a less-perfect; perfection, in Plotinian language, is always a synonym for the simplex, and we have therefore in this series the One as absolute simplex, the Intellectual-Principle as the actual simplex and logical duality; and thirdly, Soul as the immanent concept, with its unity in the One, its teleology in the Intellectual-Principle and its multiplicity in the visible universe.

'The Soul once seen to be thus precious, thus divine, you may hold the faith that by its possession you are already nearing God: in the strength of this power make upwards towards Him. At no great distance you must attain—there is not much between. But over this divine, there is a still diviner. Grasp the upward neighbour of the Soul, its prior and source. Soul, for all the worth we have shown to belong to it, is yet a secondary, an image of the Intellectual-Principle. Reason uttered is an image of the reason stored within the Soul, and in the same way Soul is an utterance of the Intellectual-Principle. It is even the total of its activity, the entire stream of life sent forth by that Principle to the production of further being . . . Its substantial existence comes from the Intellectual-Principle, and the Logos within it becomes Act in virtue of its contemplation of that prior'.[93]

This passage clearly indicates the trend of Plotinus' thought. The problem to be solved is the same as in the case of the relation between the One and the Intellectual-Principle—there must be differentiation without separation. Now and then he seeks the aid of symbolic language in his attempt to reach clarity. There must be an entity generating without volition and without any resultant change in the generating entity. 'Imagine a spring that has no source outside itself; it gives itself to all the rivers, yet is never exhausted by what they take, but remains always integrally as it was; the tides that proceeds from it are at one within it before they run their several ways, yet all, in some sense, know beforehand down what channels they will pour their stream'.[94] 'We dare not talk of generation in time, dealing as we are with eternal Beings . . . it can neither have yielded assent nor uttered decrees nor stirred in any way towards the existence of a secondary'.[95]

But notwithstanding the emergence of a secondary entity, the generated entity remains within the source. The Soul works in the sphere of the Intellectual-Principle. Even divine thought, perfect self-thought, is ascribed to it. So intimate is the relation between them that the two are actually one. The characteristic act of the Soul is performed by virtue of its vision of the Intellectual-Principle. The identity-in-diversity of the Neo-Platonistic Godhead is one of the basal theses of Plotinus. But before we discuss this in greater detail, something must be said of the nature and functions of the Soul. As the basis for our discussion we will take the following two passages from the *Enneads*.

'Let every soul recall, then, at the outset, the truth that Soul is the author of all living things, that it has breathed the life into them all, whatever is nourished by earth and sea, all the creatures of the air, the divine stars in the sky; it is the maker of the sun; itself formed and ordered this vast heaven and conducts all that rhythmic motion: and it is a principle distinct from all these to which it gives law and movement and life, and it must of necessity be more honourable than they, for they gather or dissolve as Soul brings them life or abandons them, but Soul, since it never can abandon itself, is of eternal being . . . As the rays of the sun throwing their brilliance upon a lowering cloud make it gleam all gold, so the Soul entering the material expanse of the heavens has given life, has given immortality; what was abject it has lifted up; and the heavenly system, moved now in endless motion by the Soul that leads it in wisdom, has become a living and a blessed thing . . . The Soul's nature and power will be brought out more clearly, more brilliantly, if we consider next how it envelops the heavenly system and guides all its purposes; for it has bestowed itself upon all that huge expanse so that every interval, small and great alike, all has been ensouled. The material body is made up of parts, each holding its own place, some in mutual opposition, and others variously independent; the Soul is in no such condition. Each separate life lives by the Soul entire, omnipotent in the likeness of the engendering father, entire in unity and entire in diffused variety'.[96]

'Time lay, self-concentrated, at rest within the Authentic Existent: it was not yet Time; it was merged in the Authentic and motionless with it. But there was an active principle there, one set on governing itself and realizing itself, and it chose to aim at something more than its present. It stirred from its rest, and Time stirred with it . . . For the Soul contains an unquiet faculty, always desirous of translating elsewhere what it saw in the Authentic Realm and it could not bear to retain within itself all the dense fulness of its possession. A seed is at rest. The nature-principle [λόγος] within, uncoiling outwards, makes way towards what seems to it a large life; . . . it is so with this faculty, when it produces the Kosmos known to sense—the mimic of the Divine Sphere, moving not in the very movement of the Divine but in its similitude, in an effort to reproduce that of the Divine. To bring this Kosmos into being, the Soul first laid aside its eternity and clothed itself with Time . . .'[97]

From these two passages it is clear that the Soul is the creative Logos, the Idea of the Intellectual-Principle. It is the power which has created the visible universe; it is also the power which maintains it by its immanence. And this immanence must clearly be understood in the sense of all in all and all in every part. From this thesis, that the Soul is immanent in every entity of the visible universe, flows the Plotinian theory of universal animation. He sees the sun and the stars as animate beings, gods, as he calls them, and in a graded measure it is so with all entities of the visible world.

We must, however, remember that ψυχή was for Plotinus something else than merely soul. To say that he believed in universal animation means nothing more than that it was his standpoint that the creative Logos had acted on, and in a varying degree was immanent in, all entities. That is the essential condition for the existence of any particular entity—the immanence of the Soul in matter. The visible universe, as we shall see in a later chapter, is nothing else than the replica, on a material medium, of the Cosmic Idea. Preller and Ritter[98] give the impression that in the Plotinian scheme, all things are animated, in the sense that they have a soul, or life, but it means nothing more than that every particular entity is the product of the action of form on matter.

This, then, is the first attribute of the Soul. It is immanent in the visible universe. A second attribute is that it is divine.

Plotinus leaves us in no doubt that the Soul is one of the three hypostases of the Godhead. It is intimately associated with the Intellectual-Principle. Plotinus knows of no sharp lines of demarcation, neither between God and creation nor between the hypostases of the Godhead. At most we would be able to say that the Intellectual-Principle is God as a teleological concept, while the Soul is the active principle of that teleology, the λόγος σπερματικός. We have already seen that the Intellectual-Principle has vision, and that the visible universe is the unwilled product of that self-vision. It is quite clear that Plotinus often identifies the Soul with this vision. It is the Intellectual-Principle in its creative activity just as the Intellectual-Principle is the One in its teleological aspect. 'The Soul containing the Ideal-Principles [εἴδη] of Real-being and itself an Ideal-Principle—includes all in concentration within itself'.[99]

Apparently we cannot clearly distinguish between the Soul on the one hand and the Intellectual-Principle as Thought, on the other. It is the 'active principle' in the Cosmic Idea. It 'translates elsewhere what it sees in the Authentic Realm';[100] it includes all the content of the Cosmic Idea in itself.

There is, for instance, no indication whatsoever, that Plotinus regarded the Soul as one of the Ideas in the Intellectual-Principle, as νοητά. There is, actually, no indication in the *Enneads* that Plotinus ever attempted to disintegrate the νοητά into separate ideas. There is for him but one idea, the Cosmic Idea, a unity-in-actuality and a plurality-in-potentiality. It is stated quite clearly that the Intellectual-Principle is an absolute unity where the only duality consists

E

in the distinction between thought and object of thought. How, then, would such a unity be subdivided and the name *Soul* be given to one portion? What is more, our last citation clearly states that the Soul contains the ideas of entities. It is therefore nothing else than the Intellectual-Principle as λόγος σπερματικός. And that is exactly what we would expect of the immanent phase of the Ultimate Reality.

One thing more we would expect of such immanence: namely that it must be the link between the Absolute and the Particular, between God and Creation. And the *Enneads* give the answer in no uncertain way. 'Soul has something of the lower on the body side and something of the higher on the side of the Intellectual-Principle'.[101]

Here, then, we have a logical substitute for the illogical God in the Timaios of Plato. [The mediator between the Absolute and the creation is found in the Soul, which is at once There and Here.] 'All that is Divine Intellect will rest eternally above, and could never fall from its sphere, but, poised entire in its own high place, will communicate to things here through the channel of Soul'.[102] 'But the Soul borders also upon the sun of this sphere, and it becomes the medium by which all is linked to the over-world'.[103]

[The result is that God and His creation constitute a unity where every entity shares in the nature of the entity immediately preceding it, from the lowest manifestation of form in matter to the transcendence of the Absolute in its nature of the One.] 'Everything brought into being under some principle not itself is contained either within its maker or, if there is any intermediate, within that; having a prior essential to its being, it needs that prior always, otherwise it would not be contained at all. It is the order of nature—the last in the immediately preceding lasts, and so thing within thing up to the very pinnacle of source'.[104]

[ The Soul is therefore a complex entity. Not only does it remain eternally identical with the Intellectual-Principle, but it is also the active Logos of that Principle immanent in nature. It is the link between the Absolute and the Particular. ] ⅃ + ᛈ 67

then 60

## Are the Three Hypostases One?

We are now in a position to discuss this question in more detail. It is my standpoint that the three hypostases of the Plotinian Godhead are merely aspects of the same Being, and that we are entitled to describe that Being by the name of one of the three hypostases, according to the nature or activity to which we are referring. I have already drawn attention to the fact that it is logically impossible to regard the One as an independent entity. I have also referred to the actual identity of the One and the Intellectual-Principle, and passages from the *Enneads* have been cited to prove that they are the transcendence and teleology, respectively, of the Godhead. I have already adduced some evidence that the Intellectual-Principle and the Soul are one. I shall discuss further passages from the *Enneads* in their bearing on this problem.

The first passage I have found in the apparently unimportant tractate which Porphyrius, when he arranged the works of Plotinus, was apparently at a loss to classify, and which appears in the *Enneads* under the title 'Detached Considerations'.[105] In the first portion of this tractate Plotinus discussed the Intellectual-Principle as the ultimate cause of creation. After postulating the unity of the Principle, he says: 'The Cosmic Idea [τὸ νοητόν] is the Intellectual-Principle [νοῦς] in its repose, unity, immobility. The Intellectual-Principle, contemplator of that content—of the Intellectual-Principle thus in repose—is an active manifestation of the same Being, an Act which contemplates its unmoved phase and, as thus contemplating, stands as Intellectual-Principle [νοῦς] to that of which it has the intellection: it is Intellectual-Principle in virtue of having that intellection, at the same time it is Intellectual Object [νοητόν], by assimilation. This, then, is the Being which planned to create in the lower Universe what it saw existing in the Supreme, the four orders of living beings. No doubt the *Timaios* seems to imply tacitly that this planning Principle is distinct from the other two: but the three—the Essentially Living [τὸ ζῷον αὐτὸ ὅ ἐστιν, the Cosmic Idea, or the νοητά], the Intellectual-Principle [νοῦς] and the planning Principle—will, to others, be manifestly one. The truth is that, by a common accident, a particular trend of thought has occasioned the discrimination.

'We have dealt with the first two; but the third—this Principle which decided to work upon the things contemplated by the Intellectual-Principle in the Essentially-Living, to create them, to establish them in their partial existence—what is this third? Is it possible that in one aspect the Intellectual-Principle is the principle of partial existence, while in another aspect it is not? The entities thus particularized from the unity are products of the Intellectual-Principle, which thus would be, to that extent, the separating agent. On the other hand it remains within itself, indivisible; division begins with its offspring which, of course, means with Souls. And thus Soul—with its particular souls—may be the separative principle. This is what is conveyed where we are told that the separation is the work of the third Principle and begins within the third. For to this third belongs the discursive reasoning which is no function of the Intellectual-Principle, but characteristic of its secondary, of Soul, to which precisely, divided by its own kind, belongs the act of division'.[106]

What Plotinus means is clear enough. The Intellectual world, as νοῦς and νοητά, as Thinking Principle and as Cosmic Content, does not *per se* explain the particular entities of the visible universe. Consequently he postulates a third principle, which practically takes the place of the Creator in the *Timaios* and which, as planning and separating agents and as 'creator judged that all the content of that essentially living Being must find a place in this lower universe also'.[107]

But is it not, perhaps, a Principle which is derived from the Intellectual-Principle and consequently stands apart from it? Plotinus answers this question in no uncertain language. 'The three, the Essentially Living, The Intellectual-Principle, and this Planning Principle will, to others, be manifestly one. The truth is that, by a common accident, a particular trend of thought has occasioned the discrimination'.[108]

Clearly it is the standpoint of Plotinus that the Soul is an inherent phase of the Intellectual-Principle.

The second passage is even more explicit. In his discussion of the relation of the Intellectual-Principle to the Soul, he says: 'Is the Soul, even in the Intellectual Realm, under the dispensation of a variety confronting it and a content of its own? No: once pure in the Intellectual, it too possesses that same unchangeableness; for it possesses identity of essence. When it is in that region it must of necessity enter into oneness with the Intellectual-Principle by the sheer fact of its self-orientation, for by that intention all interval disappears. The Soul advances and is taken into unison, and in that association becomes one with the Intellectual-Principle, but not to its own destruction. The two are one, and two. In such a state there is no question of stage and change. The Soul, without motion (but by right of its essential being) would be intent upon its intellectual act, and in possession, simultaneously, of its self-awareness. For it has become one simultaneous existence with the Cosmic Idea [νοητόν]'.[109]

The importance of this passage is that it grants the Soul that very trait which is the distinctive essence of the Intellectual-Principle, namely immediate self-knowledge without any reference to externa. The two hypostases have one simultaneous existence: they are one and two. That they are one he states in the cited passage. How they can at the same time be two, he explains in the next paragraph, where he goes on to show that the Soul creates and that it is immanent in creation.

Plotinus could hardly have been more explicit. The two concepts are distinguished but not separate. They are, in other words, aspects of the same entity. 'Three persons, but one substance', are the words of the well-known Christian *symbolon*. Plotinus means the same thing: the two are one and two.

A name is less than a description. It is nothing more than a brief formula. The second hypostases, the Intellectual-Principle is, as we have seen, self-intent self-knowing thought. And just that, according to Plotinus in the cited passage, is also the Soul.

Had it not been for the fact that commentators of Plotinus without any exception regard the Plotinian Godhead as a graded Triad, where the One is the author of the Intellectual-Principle and that Principle the author of the Soul and that there are grades of majesty and power in the three hypostases, I would have been content to regard the proofs I have adduced as conclusive. Under the circumstances I believe that the evidence of further citations from the *Enneads* is necessary.

The following passage needs preliminary explanation. As MacKenna[110] correctly says, the names Ouranios, Kronos, and Zeus are sometimes used by Plotinus to denote respectively the One, the Intellectual-Principle and the Soul. Here he speaks of the knowledge which Zeus, i.e. the Soul, has of his own activities as creative Logos. 'Zeus will know all to be one thing existing in virtue of one life for ever: it is in this sense that the All is unlimited, and thus Zeus' knowledge of it will not be as of something seen from outside but as of something embraced in true knowledge, for this unlimited thing is an eternal indweller within himself, or, to be more accurate, eternally follows upon him . . . Zeus knows his own unlimited life, and, in that knowledge, knows the activity that flows from him to the Kosmos. But he knows it in his unity, not in its process'.[111]

Here again the attributes of the Intellectual Principle are transferred to the Soul. It acts immediately, and we know that immediate knowledge is the essence of the Intellectual-Principle, while the Soul is essentially an immanent, creative principle, acting discursively and mediately. Here he plainly says that Zeus knows his own content immediately. That content, because it is the object of immediate knowledge, must be the Cosmic Idea, the νοητά. As in the first passages cited in this chapter, so here the Soul is identified with the Nous, the Intellectual-Principle as Thought, where the object of that thought or vision, the Cosmic Content or νοητά, is immediately known. 'He knows it in its unity, not in its process'.

Plotinus goes on to say that 'the ordering principle is twofold. There is the principle known to us as the Demiurgos and there is the soul of the All. We apply the appellation Zeus sometimes to the Demiurgos and sometimes to the principle conducting the universe. When under the name of Zeus we are considering the Demiurgos we must leave out all notions of stage and progress, and recognize one unchanging and timeless life. But the life in the Kosmos, the life which carries the leading principle of the universe, still needs elucidation. Does it operate without calculation, without searching into what ought to be done? Yes: for what must be stands shaped before the Kosmos, and is ordered without any setting in order'.[112]

This passage is very important. The third aspect in the Intellectual-Principle to which we referred at the beginning of this section, in other words the Active-Principle or Soul (see *Ennead* III. 9, 1) is one with the Intellectual-Principle. It is the Soul. But while that Soul is regarded in its character of immanence, the Soul as Active Principle of the Intellectual-Principle is without stage or change. It possesses a timeless and unchanging life. It is only the lower phase of the Active or Planning Principle which is immanent in the universe. It is, as we have seen, within the sphere of Time. It is discrete in the discrete entities of the visible universe. In his discussion of the relation of time, and eternity, Plotinus says that 'the origin of Time, clearly, is to be traced to the first stir of the Soul's tendency towards the production of the sensible universe with the consecutive act ensuing'.[113] But we have already seen from the passages already cited [114] that Time is not inherent in the Soul which is the Active Principle in the Cosmic World. What is more, to the higher phase of the Soul Plotinus attributes only those traits which are of the essence of the Intellectual-Principle.

My explanation of these facts is as follows. Plotinus, as Idealist, knows of no clear lines of demarcation. There is no gulf between God and creation. The Godhead is a trinity in the sense that the three aspects are one entity, although certain aspects are more primal than others. Notwithstanding the clear logical distinction between those phases, there is no separation. The temptation to attempt a graphic representation of these entities is as great as it is dangerous, but the attempt of Plotinus to represent the relation as circles within circles[115] is very illustrative, although essentially dangerous. The fact that the Intellectual-Principle and the Soul are one is emphasized by granting them the same attributes, while the distinction between them is made clear by postulating the discrete activity of the lower and immanent aspect of the planning Principle. The question of the relation between the different phases of the Soul will be discussed in detail at a later stage; here I can say that, although there is distinction between these phases, there is no question of separation.

That the Soul consists of phases or aspects, is repeatedly stated by Plotinus. 'There is also the decided difference that Nature operates toward the Soul, and receives from it; Soul, near to Nature, but superior, operates towards Nature but without receiving in turn; and there is the still higher phase, with no action whatever upon body or upon Matter'.[116]

There is one difficulty which needs explanation. In III. 7 it is very clearly stated that Eternity or rather Timelessness is a characteristic of the Intellectual-Principle, as Time is of the Soul. If, then, the Intellectual-Principle and the Soul are one, on what grounds are we entitled to distinguish between them with reference to Time and Timelessness? Plotinus gives the following answer: 'Can we escape by the theory that, while human souls—receptive of change, even to the change of imperfection and lack—are in time, yet the Soul of the All, as the author of time, is itself timeless? But if it is not in time, what causes it to engender time rather than eternity? The answer must be that the realm it engenders is not that of eternal things, but a realm of things enveloped in time. It is just as the souls are not in time, but some of their experiences and productions are. For Soul is eternal, and is before Time'.[117]

In other words, we must distinguish between Soul and its products. The Soul and the Intellectual-Principle are one entity, but different aspects. The activity of the Soul goes beyond the Cosmic Idea in the visible universe, or, to put the matter in different words, God, in his teleological aspect remains the unmoved archetype or plan of the universe, but God, as immanent Principle by whom all things are made, does not remain unmoved, but immanates in the entities of the time-space sphere.

In the very next paragraph Plotinus tackles the whole problem of the relation of the three hypostases to one another. I quote *in extenso*.

'But if in the Soul thing follows thing, if there is earlier and later in its productions, if it engenders or creates in time; then it must be looking towards the future, and if towards the future, then towards the past as well? No; prior and past are in the things it produces; in itself nothing is past. All, as we have said, is one simultaneous grouping of Logoi. In the engendered, dissimilarity is not compatible with unity, though in the Logoi supporting the engendered, such unity of dissimilars does occur—hand and foot are in unity in the Logos [of man] but apart in the realm of sense. Of course, even in that ideal realm there is apartness, but in a characteristic mode, just as in a mode, there is priority. Now, apartness may be explained as simply differentiation. But how account for priority unless on the assumption of some ordering principle, arranging from above, and in that disposal necessarily affirming a serial order?' In other words, Plotinus here asks whether the hypostases are a gradation. Modern commentators have answered this question in the affirmative. The answer of Plotinus is illustrative. He proceeds: 'There must be such an ordering principle, but the indicated conclusion does not follow unless order and ordering principle are distinct. If the ordering principle is Primal Order, there is no such affirmation of series: there is simply making, the making of this thing after that thing. The affirmation would imply that the ordering principle looks away towards Order, and therefore is not itself Order. But how are Order and this orderer one and the same? Because the ordering principle is no conjoint of matter and idea, but is soul, pure idea, the power and energy, second only to the Intellectual-Principle . . . The total scheme may be summarized in the illustration of the Good [i.e. the One] as a centre, the Intellectual Principle as an unmoving circle, the Soul as a circle in motion'.[118]

Plotinus here struggles with the problem to reconcile unity and diversity in the Absolute. There must be distinction and even priority in a way, and yet he stresses the impossibility of a gradation in the Godhead. It is the same problem which Christianity in the first four centuries struggled to solve. We have already seen that Plotinus declared the two to be one and the one, two. Here he solves the problem by pointing out that, if the ordering principle is the One, there can be no gradation, because Order and the ordering principle are one, and that order is diffuse over the whole Ideal World. The Godhead is order. That order is the unifying principle—the One. The One is therefore an attribute of the whole Godhead.

And if the One is an attribute or phase of the whole Godhead, it must be so also in the case of the other two hypostases. Attributes are distinguished from one another but not separated. We cannot abstract an attribute of an entity and then call that attribute an entity with priority over other abstracted attributes.

What, then, are our conclusions? The Soul is the life of God, just as the One is his transcendence and the Intellectual-Principle his teleology. This life of God is at the same time also the life of the universe, but here we find it in its lower or immanent phase, lower because it has come into contact with time-space spheres. God and His life cannot be separated. The Neo-Platonic Godhead without the Soul would have been unthinkable. And yet it is not a part of God. It is God.

Just as the Intellectual-Principle is, viewed from different standpoints, beauty, truth, etc., so God, viewed from another standpoint, is life, teleology and transcendence. The three are one and the one, three. All life is Psyche or the Life, but all life is not equally close to the source of Life, which is God.

I believe I have said enough to prove that the accepted interpretation of the Plotinian Godhead is incorrect. We are not justified in regarding the three hypostases as a gradation of three persons, where there are grades of power and majesty. It would, in the first place, be logically impossible. We have already touched on that matter in our discussion of the One. In the second place, the accepted interpretation is contrary to the clear verdict of the *Enneads*.

I need not enlarge on the importance of my thesis. If my interpretation is correct, Plotinus is one of the most logical and acceptable interpreters of the Being of God whom the world has ever seen. There is hardly any disagreement between the Plotinian and the Christian interpretations of this matter, and what difference there is I would formulate as follows: The Christian interpretation is, unavoidably perhaps, in certain respects anthropomorphic. I say unavoidably, because it is in the first place a theology and not a philosophical system. I have no hesitation in saying that no religion or theology with a universal appeal could dispense with anthropomorphic elements. But apart from this, I can see no profound difference between Neo-Platonism and Christianity except, perhaps, for the particularized incarnation of the Logos. I say particularized, for the incarnation of the Logos is also Plotinian. The words of St. John, ὁ λόγος σὰρξ ἐγένετο, would, perhaps, in Plotinus have been ὁ λόγος σὰρξ γέγονεν, in order to disassociate that incarnation from the particular person and the particular moment in time. But nothing more.

Many questions remain to be answered before we will be in a position to judge Plotinus as religious teacher. These questions, together with the problem of Plotinus' attitude to incarnation, will be dealt with in later portions of this work.

### Creation

The Soul, as we have already seen, although it is one with the Intellectual-Principle and in its higher phase has no dealings with the space-time spheres, nevertheless becomes the discursive immanent principle which is the creative activity of God. God's life, which is God Himself, becomes the life of all existing entities, although in the space-time sphere that divine life comes into contact with matter, and is therefore not the pure concept as found in the Ideal World.

This is the basis of the Plotinian theory of creation, and with it coincides his concept of universal animation which at first may seem strange to us, until we remember that ψυχή means for Plotinus life in the sense of participation in the divine. Even the lowest entity in the visible universe would, by virtue of its very existence, participate in the Cosmic Idea, and universal animation means little more than that the temporal exists by virtue of the eternal and that God is immanent in all creation.

To regard the Soul as the link between God and the universe is a common view of Plotinian commentators, and there is nothing to be said against that interpretation. But the Soul must on no account be regarded as a mediator between God and man. It has nothing in common with the second Person in the Christian Trinity. There is more affinity with the Holy Spirit, because both concepts can be regarded as the immanent phases of the Godhead. The Soul is the link between the Universal and the Particular in the sense that it is, in relation to the universe, the indwelling God, and that, by virtue of that indwelling, all entities in the universe have their being.

In his discussion of the *modus quo* of creation, Plotinus first deals with the theories that there is no Creator; secondly, that the Creator is evil; and thirdly, that the Creator had consciously created in time.

In other words, his polemic is directed against Atheism, Gnosticism and the theistic religions of which Christianity, in the time of Plotinus, was the most important. He wastes little time on Atheism. 'To make the existence and coherent structure of this Universe depend upon automatic activity, and upon chance, is against all good sense. Such a notion could be entertained only where there is neither intelligence nor even ordinary perception, and reason enough has been urged against it, though none is really necessary'.[119]

His refutation of Gnosticism will be dealt with in a separate section of this chapter. His most important objection to that system is not its Christology; and in the tractate concerned[120] I can find no bitter polemic against Christianity, although Inge[121] seems to think there is.

The Christian view of creation in time is for Plotinus an impossible thesis, because God in that case would not be God. If He had created the universe at some particular stage, why not earlier or later? Clearly because something influenced or moved Him at that period, and that unknown something would then be co-existent with God.

'But since we hold the eternal existence of the Universe, the utter absence of a beginning to it, we are forced, in sound and sequent reasoning, to explain the providence ruling in the Universe as an universal consonance with the divine Intelligence to which the universe is subsequent not in time but in the fact of derivation, in the fact that the Divine Intelligence preceding it in kind, is its cause as being the Archetype and Model which it merely images, the primal by which, from all eternity, it has the existence and subsistence'.[122]

In other words, the Intellectual-Principle is the *causa finalis*, the teleological archetype, of which the universe is but the image. It is indeed strange how this very passage has been misused, even by Inge[123] who, in his comment on it, declares that according to Plotinus 'matter has been created, but not in time'. To confuse the visible universe with the Neo-Platonic ὕλη or Matter, is, of course, utterly wrong. Matter is the negation of all being. How can that which is not, be created? What we, in modern language, call matter is Plotinian matter or ὕλη, with form or λόγος of the Soul superimposed. And that Soul is one with the life of God. The visible universe is therefore a compound of two uncreated factors, τὸ ὄντως ὄν or Divine Soul, and τὸ μὴ ὄν or Matter.

The Intellectual-Principle is, then, the teleological archetype of the Universe. But there is no action or volition in that Principle with reference to the creation of the world. As absolute self-contemplator, the Intellectual-Principle would not even be aware of the existence of the lower entities. But here again, a word of warning would not be amiss. When we speak of the Intellectual-Principle we speak of a phase of the Ultimate Reality and nothing more. To say that the Intellectual-Principle did not exercise any action or volition with reference to the creation of the universe, means nothing more than that the Ultimate Reality in its capacity as pattern, remained unmoved. In its capacity as immanent, creative force, it reflected on Matter, the image of itself. 'God created man in his image'. That archetype remained unchanged, but only by a logical abstraction can we say that God as the archetype, the *causa finalis*, did not will or act in creation. The God who wills and the God who is the pattern, is one Being. The Ultimate Reality is one. The νοητά, the Cosmic Idea, is eternally unchanged. We have heard of the categories of Being, Identity, Rest. The Cosmic Idea is the same to-day, yesterday and for ever. 'But such is the blessedness of this Being [The Intellectual-Principle] that in its very non-action it magnificently speaks and in its self-dwelling it produces mightily . . . The Kosmos of parts exists not as a result of a judgment establishing its desirability, but by the sheer necessity of a secondary kind'.[124]

Inge is therefore wrong when he says that 'matter was created in order that the will-activities of Soul and Spirit [i.e. the Intellectual-Principle] might become actualities'.[125] Matter was never created, because it is the negation of Being. Nor are there will-activities of the Soul and the Intellectual-Principle. The only activity of the

Intellectual-Principle is self-contemplation, which is, as Arnou[126] calls it, the λόγος μένων, the non-active Logos.

What is contemplation? It is dynamic and productive. It is divine action, or, to express it better, action is human contemplation. Let us tackle this problem from the human angle. What happens when I act? In the first place, I see, I contemplate the desired end. But because my vision is barren and vain, I attempt, by the laborious time-space method of action, to realize that vision. Even in the very highest spheres of our creative activities, that is the case. The conception and birth of a child, the outpouring of an artist's soul on canvas or in music, the expression in words of our adoration of God—in every case recourse must be had to action, because our mere contemplation or vision is barren. The heart may be pregnant with an idea, a vision, but the realization of that vision is a travail of the space-time-bound human creator. And ever the result falls short of the vision. Did the religious mystic, Thomas à Kempis, succeed in expressing to the full his profound love and adoration of God? Is the music in the heart of the composer not more satisfying, more perfect, than his vision realized? Is poetry in truth 'the spontaneous overflow of mighty feeling'? Or is it but the echo? Is it but the lava forced out of profound depths by even deeper powers which never see the light? Is the human creator ever satisfied? How could he be, since it is the God in him who sees, while his time-space-bound human hands are his only tools with which to realize, in time-space-bound matter, his vision of spheres where space and time are not? While I am writing these pages, I experience what I say and within my human limitations, I attempt to render imperfectly in space-bound language truths which transcend my powers or the power of human words.

With God it is otherwise. Proclus has said that in the case of God volition and necessity are identical.[127] We cannot speak of volition with reference to the Intellectual-Principle, but we can say that contemplation and necessity are there identical. The Nous contemplates the Cosmic Idea, and the image, the Universe, is the product.

We must remember that we are here dealing with the concept of eternal creation. The Eternal Nous eternally contemplates the Eternal Cosmic Idea, and the visible universe is eternally the image reflected on Matter, the eternal non-Being. We need not be unduly concerned, like Inge, with the problem of Matter. Plotinus does not, as Inge[138] seems to imply, hold that creation consists in shaping matter. Plotinian matter is not material, in the modern sense of the word. In a later chapter I shall enlarge on this, but there can be no question of the 'creation' of τὸ μὴ ὄν. Such a thesis would be a contradiction in terms. The visible world is material because it is partially unreal.

The objection may perhaps be made that, if the universe comes into existence by virtue of the vision of the Intellectual-Principle, there is no necessity for the existence of the Soul. There are two answers to the objection. In the first place we must remember that Plotinus has already identified the Soul with its Active phase, the Nous. The Soul is the Intellectual-Principle in its creative imma-nence, just as the One is that Principle in its transcendent unity. The Ultimate Reality is a one-in-many. The many can be abstracted only logically, not actually. And in the second place we must remember that the vision of the Intellectual-Principle, in its creative phase, in other words, the activity of the Soul, is a progressive and decreasing concept. It is the life of God which is eternally given to the next entity, and so on in ever decreasing measure.

From the source, the Intellectual-Principle, down to the lowest entity, the series will be as follows: First, there is the Intellectual-Principle, which, in its character as the Soul, is the circumactive life of God.[129] This principle, as we have seen, is, as Life, one with God, and at the same time it is immanent in the universe. It is, in other words, the measure of the Life of God present in these entities which have come into being as a result of the vision of the Nous. Zeller correctly speaks of the *dynamischen Pantheismus* of Plotinus.[130] I say correctly, because Plotinus nowhere attempts to draw a line of demarcation between this life as being purely divine and its manifestation in creation.

This Soul, as immanent concept, is the Logos of the Universe. 'This Logos is not the Intellectual-Principle unmingled, nor does it descend from the pure Soul alone. It is a dependent of that Soul while, in a sense, it is a radiation from both those divine hypostases. Now all life, even the least valuable, is an activity, and not a blind activity like that of flame. Any object in which Life is present, any object which participates in Life, is at once enreasoned in the sense that the activity peculiar to Life is formative, shaping as it moves'.

In other words, the emerging Logos is the Life of God controlled by the teleology embodied in the content of the Cosmic Idea, the νοητά. And the result is, of course, that the universe is a unity. In minor matters there may be a clash between part and part, or, as Plotinus put it, it 'is at war with itself in the parts which it now exhibits, but it has nevertheless the unity or harmony of a drama torn with struggle. The drama, of course, brings the conflicting elements to one final harmony, weaving the entire story of the clashing characters into one thing'.[131] In the midst of all difference, there is 'one increasing purpose'. 'What is evil in the single soul will stand a good thing in the universal system. What in the unit offends nature will serve nature in the total event. Thus, even as things are, all is well'.[132]

And all is well only because there is one Ultimate Reality, one Teleology, one Divine Life, one all-transcending Unity in the midst of diversity.

But we must view this matter from yet another angle. What is the basis, the substratum, on which this Life is impressed? Life is the form, matter is the ὕλη. These concepts will be dealt with in detail in our chapter on Matter and the Visible Universe.

## 'Against the Gnostics'

The tractate against the Gnostics [133] was apparently written only with the purpose of criticizing certain aspects of Gnostic creed, but apart from that negative criticism there are certain valuable positive theses which elucidate the standpoint of Plotinus himself.

Gnosticism was the name not of a sect but of a tendency in which certain common traits were found. It was definitely un-Hellenic, but in certain respects there were Hellenic elements incorporated in their system which show a definite agreement with certain Neo-Platonic doctrines. They believed in the affinity of the Soul with God, they accepted the doctrine that the soul could never be absolutely cut off from its Creator, and that God was above Being.

Plotinus opens the tractate with an attack on the multiplicity of divine hypostases in Gnostic dogma. He proves again that there can be only three such hypostases. All thought is by its very nature directed to the attainment of a unity. In the next paragraph (II. 9, 4) he attacks those who say 'that creation is the work of the Soul after the failing of its wings. To them we give the answer that no such disgrace could overtake the Soul of the All. If they tell us of its falling, they must also tell us what caused the fall. And when did it take place? If from eternity, then the Soul must essentially be a fallen thing; if at some one moment, why not before that? We assert that its creative act is a proof not of decline but rather of its steadfast hold. Its decline could consist only in its forgetting the Divine. But if it forgot, how could it create? Whence does it create but from the things it knew in the Divine? And if it creates from the memory of that vision, it never fell. Even supposing it to be in some dim intermediate state, it need not be supposed more likely to decline. Any inclination would be towards its prior, in an effort to the clearer vision. If any memory at all remained, what other desire could it have than to retrace the way?'

Nor is Plotinus prepared to accept the doctrine that the Creator of the Universe is evil and that the strife and contradictions in the visible universe are to be explained by that cause. 'Nor may we grant that this world is of unhappy origin because there are many jarring things in it. Such a judgment would rate it too high, treating it as the same with the Intelligible Realm, and not merely its reflection'.[134] Logically nothing can be said against this criticism of Plotinus. Only the total, the whole, which is God, can be perfect.

But his most important objection against the Gnostics is that, while they claim to be in contact with God, they refuse to admit that the sun and the stars also have that contact. This criticism was probably based on a misunderstanding. Neither Plotinus nor the Gnostics ever meant that the heavenly bodies had souls, in our sense of that word. The term 'ensouled', or 'animated' meant for Plotinus little more than the measure in which the entity so styled participates in the Reality which is God. And that 'we, the late born, hindered by so many cheats in the way towards the Truth',[135] could share in that Reality more than the heavenly bodies, was for Plotinus an impossible and unacceptable doctrine. In their symmetry, discipline and order he sees proof that the Life, or ψυχή of God, lives in them to a degree greater than in us.

Plotinus also found in the Gnostics strong leanings towards materialism. 'How could any form or degree of Life come about by a blend of the elements? This conjunction could produce only a warm or cold or an intermediate substance, something dry or wet or intermediate. Besides, how could such a soul be a bond holding the four elements together, if it is a later thing and arises from them'.[136]

His quarrel is here undoubtedly with the doctrine found among certain Gnostics that we assimilate evil through the food we take, but in reality that is more asceticism than materialism.

His next criticism is probably directed against Christian Gnostics. 'These teachers in their contempt for this creation and this earth, proclaim that another earth has been made for them into which they are to enter when they depart. Now this new earth is the Logos of our world. Why should they desire to live in the archetype of a world abhorrent to them?'[137] Plotinus wrongly ascribes their errors to a mistaken interpretation of Plato. These doctrines, with few exceptions, were taken over from Oriental, Semitic or Christian sources. Gnosticism was Hellenistic, but certainly not Hellenic.

Inge [138] rightly says that it was not Greek to allow the mythological imagination to run riot in serious thinking, and that was undoubtedly the case in Gnosticism. The relation between Greek mythology and Greek philosophy is very slight, sometimes actually hostile. Plato used the myths, but as a rule not as a substitute for logical thought, and when he did, he was usually forced to do so by his inability to express his thoughts by logical concepts.

From the evil nature of the human soul the Gnostics concluded that the creator of the Universe is evil. Plotinus' reaction to this doctrine is very strong. 'To treat the human soul as a fair presentiment of the Soul of the Universe is like picking out potters and blacksmiths and making them warrant for discrediting an entire well-ordered city'.[139] The human soul is subservient to its material concomitant, the body, but the Ideal World knows no such limitation.

The fact that the Gnostics believed that the world has neither beginning nor end and that its existence coincides with the existence of God, and that notwithstanding that doctrine they nevertheless asked the question why the Creator had created the universe, is correctly regarded by Plotinus as a contradiction in terms, because the question presupposes a beginning of the universe and represents the Creator as a Being of change, who, after a period of inactivity, suddenly creates.[140]

Nor are they on firm ground when they unduly disparage the visible universe. As Whittaker[141] correctly points out, Plotinus saw the cause of our tribulations not in the evil nature of the world, but in the fact that we stand midway between God and matter. We participate in the nature of Being and of Not-Being. The

F

world is an image of the Cosmic Idea and is therefore good. But it is merely an image and therefore not perfect.

Inge[142] wrongly says that Plotinus attacked the Gnostics because they denied the plurality of the gods and that Plotinus himself in II. 9, 9 attempted a defence of polytheism. It is quite true that in the paragraph concerned he attacks the Gnostics because they despise the θεοί. But even a superficial perusal of the paragraph makes it quite clear that by the θεοί he means not the gods, in the accepted meaning of that word, but the heavenly bodies. Speaking of God, he says: 'This Universe, too, exists by Him and looks to Him— the Universe as a whole and every god within it'.[143] In the same tractate he also says: 'On the other hand, to despise this Sphere, and the gods within it or anybody else that is lovely, is not the way to goodness . . . In the heavenly bodies there are souls, intellective, holy, much closer to the Supernal Beings than are ours. For how can this Kosmos be a thing cut off from that and how imagine the gods in it to stand apart?'[144]

In this connection Mackenna says: 'Where we meet the "gods" without any specification we are to understand according to the context, sometimes the entire Divine Order; sometimes the Divine Thoughts, the Ideas or Archetypes, sometimes exalted Beings vaguely understood to exist above man as ministers of the Supreme; sometimes the stars and the earth, thought of as divine beings; sometimes there is some vague sleepy acceptance of popular notions of the Olympian personalities'.[145]

I have little disagreement with MacKenna in this respect, although I have not, in all the pages of the *Enneads*, found any vague or definite reference to 'exalted Beings understood to exist above man as ministers of the Supreme', nor have I found any acceptance, whether sleepy or otherwise, of Olympian deities, except where, as Mac-Kenna himself acknowledged, the names of Ouranios, Kronos and Zeus are used for the One, the Intellectual-Principle and the Soul respectively, or the names of other Olympian deities are used to denote some entity in the Ultimate Reality, where the context usually raises the question of identity above all doubt.

I agree that Plotinus regarded the celestial bodies as divine beings, but only in the sense that they participate in the Soul, as all existing entities participate in the Soul, although not to the same extent. We must remember that in this tractate Plotinus attacked those Gnostics who postulated an absolute gulf between God and the

Universe. What he says to them is in effect this: 'There is no gulf. Those entities which you despise, participate in the Ideal World. They are akin to matter, but also to God. Therefore they are divine. The universe is not evil. It is good, because it is the image of the Cosmic Idea. It is not perfect, because it is merely an image'.

We need not be misled by his thesis that these celestial bodies, these 'gods' are intellective [ψυχαὶ νοεραί]. He does not by that wish to convey that they are endowed with discursive reason, but that they are akin to the νοητά, the content of the Cosmic Idea, and that they are the products of the vision of the Nous.

We must remember that the apple of discord between the Greek philosophers and Christian thinkers was not Greek polytheism. The fact was that the Greeks saw in the powers of nature manifestations of God and that therefore they regarded those powers as ensouled, or animated, call it what you will. But we must remember that ensouled or animated does not, in Greek thought, connote endowment with human or animal life nor with discursive reason. It only means that they are akin to the Divine Intellect, that God is immanent in them.

To attribute to Plotinus a defence of polytheism is to misunderstand utterly the basis of Plotinian thought. Surely, we have already seen that it was one of the major objections of Plotinus against the Gnostics that they accepted a multiplicity of divine hypostases. Would it not have been the height of folly had Plotinus, after voicing that objection, proceeded to defend polytheism against the Gnostics?

The real attitude of Plotinus to the gods of Olympus was one of pious unbelief. He retained names as far as possible, but he changed concepts.

## Universal Animation

In all Idealistic thought there is the danger of being misled by words instead of trusting to concepts. In the history of Greek Idealism the modern student is faced by the additional danger inherent in the tendency to translate Greek words by apparently similar words in the modern tongue. It was very late before Greek philosophy arrived at the concept of *personality*, and consequently there is no word where confusion can be so easily caused as the word ψυχή. I have, in this treatise, followed English commentators of Plotinus by rendering it as *Soul*; German writers call it *Seele*. The French speak of *l'âme*. All three translations are, of course, wrong, because the modern connotation of those words would have been a foreign concept to Greek thinkers. The word is derived from ψύχειν, which, in the first place, means *to breathe* and also *to make cold or dry*. The noun ψυχή is *breath*, and because breath is the sign of Life, it also means *life*. Only then was the word used in contrast to σῶμα, or body.

We can, of course, translate the ψυχή of Plotinus by *soul*, but unless we are on our guard, unless we remember that we are dealing with different concepts, we will find ourselves in difficulties. That is exactly what has, so far, happened, and Plotinus has been blamed for the resulting confusion. According to Plotinus all existing entities are to a certain extent in the possession of ψυχή. On the strength of that thesis, modern commentators have wrongly come to the conclusion that Plotinus regarded all existing entities as *ensouled* or *animated*. No wonder that he has often been regarded as a pantheist.

I have also translated the Plotinian ψυχή by *Soul*. A better translation for ψυχή as divine hypostasis would have been Principle of Life or Divine Life. The lower phase of that ψυχή, which Mackenna translates as All-soul, I have, as a rule, rendered by Soul of the All, or Soul of the Universe. Had it not been for the inconvenient length of the phrase, a good translation would have been 'the emerging life of God which creates immanently in the visible universe'. But Plotinus also has a third meaning for his ψυχή, namely the human psyche, and here we are to a certain extent justified in rendering it by the word *soul*, because, as will appear later when we discuss his Psychology, the terms are reasonably synonymous.

To resume: When Plotinus says that all existing entities are in possession of ψυχή, which of the three concepts does he mean? Certainly not the first, because, as we have seen, he clearly states that the Soul is eternally identical with the Intellectual-Principle. It seems to be the general impression that he means the third, or human psyche. That that is not the case is easy to prove.

In the first place it must be pointed out that the human psyche, according to Plotinus, knows no gradation. It forms a unity and a whole. One person cannot have more psyche than another. But of those entities in which the ψυχή is immanent, he says that it does not mean that ψυχή is present in every place and thing in the same degree.[146] This clearly points to the second meaning of ψυχή, in other words, the emerging, immanent, creative life of God.

An additional proof that Plotinus does not ascribe human understanding to the celestial bodies is found in the answer which he gives to those who ask whether the stars can answer our prayers or be touched by our incantations. His answer is in the affirmative. There is a mutual sympathy in the universe. All entities are akin to one another, and by virtue of that sympathy one entity influences the other. But, he asks, is not memory essential in that case? If prayers are granted through the agency of the celestial bodies, is it not essential that those celestial bodies should have memory, since our prayers are rarely answered immediately? His answer to this question is: 'With regard to prayers; there is no question of a will that grants; the powers that answer to incantations do not act by will; a human being fascinated by a snake, has neither perception nor sensation of what is happening . . . In other words, some influence falls from the being addressed upon the petitioner—or upon someone else—but that being itself, sun or star, perceives nothing at all. The prayer is answered by the mere fact that part and other part are wrought to one tone like a musical string which, plucked at one end, vibrates at the other also. Now if the vibration in a lyre affects another by virtue of the sympathy between them, then certainly in the All—even though it is constituted in contraries—there must be one melodic system. For it contains its unisons as well, and its entire content, even to those contraries, is a kinship'.[147]

We need not, at the moment, concern ourselves with the astrological views expressed in this passage. Our present task is to determine whether Plotinus ascribed qualities to the celestial bodies which coincide with the qualities of the human soul. But here he definitely says that celestial bodies have no perception nor memory. Therefore they are not ensouled or animated, in the modern sense of the word. The sympathy between entities in the universe is not a conscious affect but a spontaneous harmony which exists by virtue of the unity of the universe.

Memory and perception are necessary elements of the human psyche, and, according to Plotinus, only of the human psyche. The Ideal World sees immediately and knows no past or future. The ψυχή of the celestial bodies is therefore nothing else than the measure in which those bodies participate in the Ideal World. It is the statement of the immanence of the temporal in the eternal.

The 'soul' of the stars and of all material entities is the immanent phase of the Soul, the third hypostasis of the Plotinian Godhead. In other words, it is the Soul of the All. It is the 'form' of Aristotle, without which no material entity can exist. It is the expression of the omnipresence of God. The bare fact that an entity exists, shows that the Divine Life or ψυχή is immanent in it, and the measure of the reality of that entity is the measure of its participation in that Life.

### Astrology

The basis of the astrological convictions of Plotinus we find in the previous section of this chapter where we came to the conclusion that the Divine ψυχή or Life permeates the universe, and that by virtue of that permeation, all things are interlinked. This in itself is, of course, no strange doctrine in modern Idealistic thought.[148]

According to Plotinus astrology can mean one of two things. The first is that 'the planets in their courses actually produce not merely such conditions as poverty, wealth, health and sickness but even ugliness and beauty, and, gravest of all, vices and virtue and the very acts that spring from these qualities, the definite doings of each moment of virtue or vice . . . More absurdly still, some of them are supposed to be malicious and others to be helpful and yet the evil stars will (in certain positions) bestow favours and the benevolent act harshly.' The second trend in astrological thought, according to Plotinus is 'that the circuits of the stars indicate definite events to come but without being the cause of all that happens'.[149]

In his argument he says that the stars are either animated or not.[150] If they are not animated, they will be able to convey only material influences, and consequently the influence of different stars will not greatly differ. Apart from that, there would not be different influences from different stars, but one combined influence from all the stars, but if that were so, it would be unthinkable that an emanating physical influence could have any profound effect on psychical and ethical aspects of human life.

But, he proceeds, even if we accept as a fact that the stars have life and thought and conscious volition (we have already seen that Plotinus denies this), how could they inflict hurt on human beings who, according to this hypothesis, would be innocent of all evil intent against the celestial bodies, since (again according to this hypothesis) men would be what they are as a result of the moulding action of the stars?

Nor can they, by their position relative to other stars, become evil or benevolent. 'We must remember that invariably every star, considered in itself, is at centre with regard to some one given group and in decline with regard to another, and vice versa. And, very certainly, it is not at once happy and sad, angry and kindly . . . Like the birds of augury, the living beings of the heavens, having no lot or part with us, may strive incidentally to foreshow the future, but they have absolutely no main function in our regard'.[151]

It is clear, therefore, that Plotinus does not accept the view that the stars can be causes, but the belief must have been very strong in his time. He devotes not less than six sections of this Tractate (II. 3, 1–6) to this theory. The third century was, of course, a period of religious revival, and in such times superstition is apt to be more general than in normal periods. But it is important to note that, notwithstanding what Brehier[152] says, Plotinus here very definitely gives no indication that his system was tainted with oriental traits.

Augury was an ancient and accredited Graeco-Roman institution, and apart from its truth or otherwise, nobody would be entitled to call it oriental. What was oriental was the belief in the stars as causative agents. Its prevalence in this period was without any doubt due to the influence of the oriental Chaldeans, and it is precisely this oriental belief that Plotinus attempts to disprove.

In *Ennead* II. 3, 7 Plotinus begins with his discussion of the second alternative, namely that the stars can, in some way or other, predict the future without themselves being responsible. His standpoint definitely is that this view is not without its element of truth. 'That the circuit of the stars indicate definite events to come but without being the cause direct of all that happens, has been elsewhere affirmed, and proved by some modicum of argument'.[153]

His task is therefore more an explanation of the facts than the proof of the facts themselves. The universe, he says, is a unity. The particular is always included in some principle which is of universal application. 'But what is this comprehensive principle of co-ordination? Establish this and we have a reasonable basis for divination, not only by stars but also by birds and other animals, from which we derive guidance in our varied concerns. All things must be enchained, and the sympathy and correspondence obtaining in any one closely knit organism must exist, and most intensely, in the All'.[154]

And because the All is a unity, although every entity has it own activity, that activity is in correspondence with the activity of the All. Consequently, he argues, the fate, both past and future, of every entity, must be included in every other entity. 'And in this order the stars, as being no minor members of the heavenly system, are co-operators'.[155] That, according to Plotinus, is the metaphysical basis of astrology.

There is the danger that we may contemptuously push aside this aspect of Plotinian thought as inferior, wondering in our own minds how a thinker of his calibre could be guilty of such folly. But the theory that the history of the All is included in every entity in the All, is not an unknown standpoint. If the universe is a unity it follows that there is co-ordination, and that every entity must have an influence on every other entity. A rock falling on a planet of some other solar system many light-years distant, would be noticed by no astronomer, but if the universe is a unity it must have its influence on every other unity in the All. The influence would, in most cases, be so minute that only an all-comprehending intelligence would be able to notice it. It is again a case of Tennyson's 'little flower'.

I have two objections against Plotinus in this respect. In the first place, he has no right to abstract stars and birds, the usual media of augury, and to exclude by implication all other entities. In the second place, the fact of universal influence may be a solid basis for potential augury, but human understanding is incapable of either noticing or interpreting such influence. Only the Absolute Intelligence would be able to do that. And then it would not be necessary to look at the stars or feed fowls and inspect their entrails. Any entity, however minute, theoretically contains the history of the All, and, by virtue of the fact that the All is a unity and is governed by one common law, each entity also theoretically contains the future history of every other entity.

Quite correctly, I believe, Plotinus denies that the particular entities, e.g. the stars, are also causes. Only the All can be a cause in this sense. Everything that happens is registered by universal influence in all entities, also in the stars, and that is the basis of augury. But just as everything that happens is registered in every single entity, so also every single entity is influenced by all that happens in all entities, and not only by a single set of entities, like the celestial bodies.

But of these things, as of many others, we may say that 'there is a soul of truth in things erroneous'.

Plotinus proceeds to point out that the ψυχή or Life of God, is in the universe, and that life is the co-ordinating agent. In our treatment of the metaphysical basis of the human soul we will also deal with a problem which has some bearing on the subject under discussion, namely predestination and free will. At this stage I may already point out that Plotinus says that some of the phenomena here on earth can be explained in terms of the circuit of the stars, but others not. In the universe he finds a co-operation of stable and mobile elements, which I interpret as the forming ψυχή and the basal matter on which it impresses its image. We are therefore partially subject to the causal series of the visible kosmos and partially free in the liberty of the Life of God.

# IV

# PSYCHOLOGY

## The Struggle against Materialism

THE heritage which Plotinus received from his forerunners in connection with the struggle for preponderance between materialism and idealism, was of a varied nature. The period between Plato and Plotinus was characterized by a gradual move in the direction of materialism. The Stoic schools, which during that period were very powerful, were in their essence materialistic, a natural result of their close association with the philosophy of Heraclitus.[156] Christianity adopted more Stoic dogmas than is generally admitted, and it is mainly these two schools of thought against which Plotinus directed his attack on materialism.

As a result of the failure of Plato to bridge the gulf between his ideal and phenomenal worlds, and the resultant inability of his successors to give a satisfactory explanation of Being, Idealism in the first centuries of the Christian era was to a large extent unpopular. The Stoics found the basis of knowledge in physical sensation, and regarded reality as the object of such knowledge, namely physical existence. Even God and the soul are regarded as material entities. Plato and Aristotle postulated a psychical monism, the Stoics a material one, and even the fact that they regarded God as reason, was no return to idealism because, like all other entities, reason also was material. The human soul is a part of God. It is therefore reasonable, but nevertheless πνεῦμα, which, according to the Stoics, had a material connotation. It is πνεῦμά πως ἔχον, in other words, a material entity with a certain *habitus*.

Plotinus finds the proof for the existence of the human soul in the existence of a governing principle which uses the body as its instrument.[157] This principle is either material or immaterial. If it is material, it can be split up into its constituents. But life must of necessity be one of those constituents, inherent in either one or all of the other constituents. But matter cannot have life inherent in it, because all matter is *per se* lifeless.

But the notion that life could be the fusion of lifeless matter, is impossible, because 'the fusion of material entities cannot produce life, nor can the irrational be the author of reason'.[158]

Nor can we believe that a happy chance could have yielded such a product, because there is a directing principle, soul. How could that which reasonably directs, be itself the product of blind chance? Visible material entities exist by virtue of the activity of the divine Soul. It is therefore unthinkable that material entities could be the author of that entity by virtue of whose activity they themselves exist.

It is quite clear that he speaks of the Stoics when he says: 'Anyone who rejects this view, and holds that either atoms or some entities void of part coming together produce soul, is refuted by the very unity of soul and by the prevailing sympathy, as much as by the very coherence of the constituents. Bodily materials, in nature repugnant to unification and to sensation, could never produce unity or self-sensitiveness, and Soul is self-sensitive. And again, constituents void of part could never produce body or bulk'.[159]

It can, however, be said that matter is a simple concept and not complex, and that soul came into existence when matter came under the influence of a formative idea,[160] by which Plotinus undoubtedly means the λόγος σπερματικός of the Stoics.

But, says Plotinus, this formative principle must either possess reality or not. If it possesses reality, the soul does not consist of the junction of that principle with matter, but it is that principle. And if it does not possess reality, he fails to understand how the change can have life as its product, 'because matter does not mould itself to pattern or bring itself to life'.[161]

Plotinus therefore comes to the conclusion that 'since neither matter nor body in any mode has this power, life must be brought upon the stage by some directing principle, external and transcendent to all that is corporeal'.[162]

The Stoic view which Plotinus attacks, is that soul is merely πνεῦμα with a certain *habitus*—πνεῦμα πως ἔχον. The concept is in Greek thought always materialistic,[163] and the doubt has been expressed whether the πνεῦμα and πνευματικοί of St. Paul are to be understood in a materialistic or semi-materialistic sense. It is, however, a fact that in later Christian thought πνεῦμα shows more affinity with the ψυχή of Neo-Platonism than with the Stoic concept.

The unity of the percipient is the basis of a number of further arguments adduced by Plotinus. 'There can be no perception without a unitary percipient whose identity enables it to grasp an object as an entirety. The several senses will each be the entrance point of many diverse perceptions; in any one object there may be many characteristics; any one organ may be the channel of a group of objects, as for instance a face is known not by a special sense for separate features, nose, eyes, etc., but by one sense observing all in one act'.[164]

Nor would a materialistic soul have memory. If sense-impressions are permanent and the soul material, no new impressions would be possible on the occupied ground, or otherwise, with the arrival of new impressions, the old would automatically disappear. Even the fact that we are capable of feeling pain, is a proof of the immaterial nature of the human soul. Take, for example, a pain in the finger. How do we feel it? The Stoic standpoint was that the semi-material πνεῦμα of which the soul consists, passes on the sensation. At first the πνεῦμα in the finger suffers and so forth, until the centre of consciousness is reached. Plotinus objects to this theory on the ground that there would then be an innumerable number of pains, one at every point at which it is passed on. And the centre of consciousness would not feel the pain in the finger, but only the pain as it arrives in its final stage. The person would, as a matter of fact, not be aware of the pain in the finger. We must therefore postulate an entity which is 'identical to itself at any and every spot'.[165]

## The Metaphysical Basis of the Human Soul

We have seen that Plotinus denies the possibility of a material origin for the human soul. Nor does he agree with those who, with an appeal to Plato, postulate but one soul with the individual soul as merely parts of the lower phase of the All-Soul, without any own identity. According to this view, the All-Soul cares for all the ensouled, and nothing of a later origin would therefore stand apart from it.[166]

The objection that Plotinus raises against this view is that, if there were only one Soul, and if that Soul were in all things, it would not be in the relation of a portion of that All-Soul in every entity, but the entire All-Soul in every particular entity'. The reasonable conclusion would then be that there would be only one identical soul, and that every separate manifestation would be that soul complete'.[167] Soul is not a quantity and consequently there can be on division. If, for instance, we were to regard the All-Soul as a numeric quantity of which every individual soul is a part, the All-Soul would consist of non-souls.

Even the analogy of science, with its particular theorems, does not satisfy Plotinus, because in a relation of that character, the All-Soul, of which the particular soul would then be a constituent, would itself not be the soul of something, not even of the universe.[168] It would have been the archetype of soul, the ideal soul, and therefore a universal, not a particular concept. And it would involve a fallacy to regard the cosmic soul as a universal entity. As Soul of the universe it is a particular soul. To make it universal would be to make it its own archetype.

Plotinus also takes into consideration the view that 'the particular souls are parts of the All-Soul in the sense that the latter bestows itself on all living things of the visible universe',[169] but his objection to this is that there could then be no question of division. The individual soul could not be called a portion of the All-Soul. It would have to be the same soul everywhere present, and everywhere present in its totality. And this is indeed the basis of the Plotinian view of the nature of Soul. Soul-kind is a unity.

That this is so, can be seen in the first place in the human soul. 'That the Soul of every individual is one thing we deduce from the fact that it is present at every point in the body—the sign of true unity—not some part of it here and another part there'.[170]

Plotinus finds proofs of this unity in almost all the phenomena of human life. The unity of our perception, thought, memory and emotion demands that this should be the case.

But also the supposition that all souls belong to the soul-kind and that we are therefore entitled to speak of the unity of soul in general, is not alien to Plotinus. To explain this thesis we must note that the Plotinian differentiation between ψυχή and ψυχῇ εἶναι,[171] in other words, the question whether there is a difference between the individual soul and essential soul, or soul-kind. The philosopher readily grants that the human soul is involved in things like sensual perception, discursive reasoning and human thought, which 'are alien to Soul'.[172] But, in fact, those things have nothing to do with soul as such. They have merely to do with soul in its relation to body [χρωμένη σώματι].[173] Soul and soul-kind are therefore of the same essence. And if that is the case, we must accept the unity of the soul and even of the individual souls in their relation to one another.

But what, then, of the fact that an independent entity must either be divided or distinguished from other entities, and that the individuality of the human soul is lost if the individual human soul is the same as soul in general, or soul-kind?

Plotinus answers the first question by pointing out that we are not allowed to apply the attributes of the embodied world to spiritual values; when an embodied entity is present in more than one independent entity, it follows that there must be division and absolute distinction between the parts of that entity so present. But soul is not subject to division. 'There are, we hold, things primarily apt to partition, tending by sheer nature towards separate existence . . . But to this order is opposed Essence [οὐσία]. This is in no degree susceptible to partition; it is unparted and impartible; interval is foreign to it, cannot enter our idea of it. It has no need of place and is not, in diffusion or as an entirety, situated within any other being; it is poised over all beings at once, and this is not in the sense of using them as a base, but in their being neither capable nor desirous of existing independent of it'.[174]

Plotinus attempts to solve the problem in the following way. The soul is divisible only in the sense that it is in every part of the entity in which it is present, but is indivisible in the sense that it is present totally in every part of that entity.[175]

I cannot agree with Inge[176] where he says that Plotinus is here under the influence of the Timaois of Plato who finds between the divisible and the indivisible a τρίτον εἶδος where all the contradictions are reconciled. In reality Plotinus here says nothing more than that soul, essentially indivisible, is indivisible in the sense that it is found in independent entities, because it exists in its full power not only in the entity as a whole, but in every part.

Neither is Plotinus prepared to grant that the unity of soul-kind precludes human individuality. 'The unity of soul, mine and another's, is not enough to make the two totals of soul and body identical. An identical thing in different recipients will have different experiences'.[177]

We can summarise the conclusions of Plotinus with reference to the unity of soul as follows. The soul is essentially a unity, although individual embodied souls retain their individuality. This problem of the unity-in-diversity is a difficult one, and it is clear that Plotinus is at a loss to explain all its aspects. Embodied souls remain individual souls by virtue of the diversity of the recipients, but that tells us nothing of the individuality or otherwise of soul as such, or un-

embodied soul or souls. It were too much to expect from Plotinus
a solution of a problem which we moderns have not yet solved.
Plotinus barely mentions the major problem. He says: 'Soul; we
must place at the crest of the world of beings, this other principle,
not merely the soul of the Universe, but, included in it, the soul of
the individual: this, no mean principle, is needed to be the bond of
union in the total of things: not, itself, a thing sprung like things
from life-seeds, but a first-hand cause, bodiless and therefore
supreme over itself, beyond the reach of cosmic causes'.[178]

Nevertheless, I believe that the solution is inherent in the system
of Plotinus. If we see in the soul of the All a soul instead of a life,
the question remains unanswered. But let us put the problem thus:
God, the highest $\psi v \chi \acute{\eta}$, gives himself to the universe. His life (the
All-Soul), creatively immanent in the universe, remains a unity,
although it is made manifest in many entities. It remains God.
The 'life' of the flower, the 'life' or form of the unensouled entity,
the soul of the human being—all these are manifested forms of one
divine life. Therefore all soul is one, because the life of one God is
immanent in all things. But nevertheless there is a necessary multiplicity. In different entities that life reacts in a different way.
Nowhere does Plotinus state this more plainly than in VI. 5, 7, where
he says: 'When we look outside of that on which we depend we
ignore our unity; looking outward we see many faces; look inward,
and all is one head. If a man could but be turned about, he would
see at once God and himself and the All'.[179]

The way in which this unity of the human soul with soul-kind is
to be explained, and the way in which the human soul came into
being, is dealt with in IV. 3. We have already pointed out that
Plotinus denies that our souls are merely parts of the All-Soul, notwithstanding the mutual unity. In this tractate he points out that
all souls are one, and yet individual unities, and the explanation of
these two apparently divergent statements is that 'soul is not subject
to division in the same way as embodied entities. Even doubters
would not agree to a division of the All-Soul, but that is precisely
what they do. They reduce the All-Soul to a logical abstraction
and think of it as they would think of wine which is divided into
many portions of the total thing called wine'.[180] In that case the
All-Soul would have as little reality as the soul of a city or a people,
which is nothing else than the combined expression of many souls
without any real transcendent unity.

This was, of course, a Neo-Pythagorean doctrine, and it amounts to a form of pantheism. All life would then be divine, but that divinity lacks a basis because there is no transcendent life. God would then be nothing else than the totality of the manifestations of life in the universe. That is the distinctive doctrine of pantheism. Idealism accepts that doctrine, with the proviso that those manifestations participate in God, and that, transcending them, is the Ideal World where the divine Life is unmixed with matter. Plotinus says: 'It is the identical soul that is present everywhere, the one complete thing, multipresent at the one moment. There is no longer question of a soul that is part, against a soul that is an all—especially when identical power is present. Even difference of function, as in eyes and ears, cannot warrant the assertion of distinct parts concerned in each separate act. All is met by the notion of one identical thing, but a thing in which a distinct power operates in each separate function'.[181]

In other words, God or Soul, is in everything. He is in the universe in the relation of whole in whole, as All-Soul, or in the relation of whole in every part, as individual Souls. The objection that this view not only makes every entity divine but also raises it to the status of God, is not well-founded, because every entity is not equally close to God. The visible universe is merely a gradation of partial being, a combination of soul and matter. For that reason not every manifestation of soul is creative. 'It is safer to say that the creative power depends on the nearness to the Ideal World'.[182]

The question arises whether Plotinus regarded the human soul as lower or higher than the soul of the Universe. The general interpretation is given by Inge,[183] who wrongly confuses the soul of the universe with the Soul as the third hypostasis of the Divine Triad. That, of course, would amount to a confusion of the transcendent and the immanent phases of God, phases that are indeed not separate but are logically yet distinct.

If the interpretation of Inge is correct, it naturally follows that the human soul is the lower entity. We have, however, clearly noticed in the previous pages of this work that the Soul, as divine hypostasis, has a higher and a lower phase, of which the first is transcendent, the latter immanent. It follows that the human soul is lower than the transcendent phase, because that phase is its source. 'The unit soul holds aloof, not actually falling into body; the differentiated souls—the All-Soul with the others—issue from the unity while still constituting, within certain limits, an association'.[184]

This passage is very clear. The All-Soul, together with the individual souls, finds its source in the transcendent Living Phase of God. In this respect they are equal.

And yet I believe that for some reason or other Plotinus attached more value to the All-Soul than to the human soul. Speaking of the Gnostics he says: 'There are men, bound to human bodies, and subject to desire, grief, anger, who think so generously of their own faculty that they declare themselves in contact with the Intelligible World, but deny that the sun possesses a similar faculty less subject to influence, to disorder, to change; they deny that it is any wiser than we, the late-born, hindered by so many cheats in the way towards truth'.[185] The following passage is very illustrative in this respect: 'But how comes it that while the All-Soul has produced a universe, the soul of the particular has not, though it is of the one ideal kind and contains, it too, all things in itself? . . . It is safer to account for the creative act by nearer connection with the over-world'.[186]

Two facts emerge very clearly. The All-Soul and the individual souls are children of the one transcendent Soul, the Living Phase of God; and in the second place, the human being stands farther away from God than the soul of the universe. And the solution to the apparent contradiction is as follows: The human soul is not a simple concept. Plotinus explicitly says that it consists of a vegetative, a rational and an intuitive phase. The vegetative phase is the lowest—it is nothing more than the manifestation of the All-Soul in the human body: the second is the essentially human phase, the distinctive attribute of the combination which Plotinus calls the ψυχὴ χρωμένη σώματι. And because it is in so intimate a contact with the body, it is bound to be of a lower calibre than the All-Soul, which is not so bound. But the third phase is the true equal of the All-Soul, in direct contact with the divine transcendent Soul.

In these three phases of the human soul we have a gradation of nearness to the divine soul. The first is, as we shall see in a later chapter, undoubtedly the natural 'sense' of Plotinian ecstasy and knowledge of God. It is practically identical with God, but is, as we shall see, not active in all men, although all men have it. The second phase is further removed from God. As a result of the limitations of the human body, or, as Plotinus calls it, the soul as

G

using a body, immediate thought and perfect self-knowledge is strange to it. The third is simply the vegetative phase that we also find in the world of plants and animals.

The answer to the question of priority in connection with the All-Soul and the human soul, will therefore depend on which phase of the human soul is meant. Soul and Soul-Kind are the same, but there are different degrees in which any particular entity can be related to soul. The human soul in its intuitive place is in immediate contact with God; in its discursive phase it is demeaned by contact with a body; in its vegetative phase it is merely a secondary manifestation of the All-Soul. The relation between the intuitive phase of the human soul and the ideal world is very intimate. 'One certain way to this knowledge (of God) is to separate first the man from the body—yourself, that is, from your body—next, to put aside that soul which moulded the body, and, very earnestly, the system of sense with desires and impulses and every such futility, all setting definitely towards the mortal: what is left is the phase of the soul which we have declared to be an image of the Divine Intellect'.[187]

Plotinus even goes further than that in stating that the highest phase of the human soul is not only an image of God, but that there is a degree of identity. 'The souls of men have entered into that realm (the visible universe) in a leap downward from the supreme; yet even they are not cut off from their origin, from the divine Intellect, it is not that they have come bringing the Intellectual Principle down in their fall; it is that though they have descended even to earth, yet their higher part holds for ever above the heavens.[188]

We have already seen, in our discussion of Intellectual Principle, that Plotinus found an actual unity between the νοῦς and the νοητά in that divine hypostasis. The νοητά are the counterparts of the Platonic ideas. In so far, therefore, as every entity here in the visible sphere has its archetype there, that entity is divine, and we have seen that Plotinus does not, like Plato, demand an ideal archetype of the ugly and the evil. The measure of divinity in the visible sphere would then depend on the measure in which the entity concerned dominates the material content of that entity. The smaller the mixture of matter, the nearer it is to God. In the intuitive phase of the human soul Plotinus finds the purest form of archetypal idea, and it is therefore grounded in the ideal world. Other entities, like the discursive soul of man, are merely the product of idea and matter— the ψυχὴ χρωμένη σώματι.

But the highest phase of the human soul is no such product. It is pure idea, a creative νοητόν. 'To know the nature of a thing we must observe it in its unalloyed state, since any addition obscures the reality. Clear, then look: or rather, let a man first purify himself and then observe: he will not doubt his immortality when he sees himself thus entered into the pure, the Intellectual. For what he sees (looking on himself) is an Intellectual Principle looking on nothing of sense, nothing of this mortality, but by its own eternity having intellection of the eternal. He will see all things in this Intellectual substance, himself having become an Intellectual Kosmos and all lightsome, illuminated by the light streaming from the Good, which radiates truth upon all that stands within that realm of the divine. Thus he will often feel the beauty of that word: 'Farewell: I am to you an immortal God', for he has ascended to the Supreme, and is all one strain to enter into likeness with it'.[189]

There is, therefore, no separation between the different manifestations of soul. The Divine Soul manifests itself as the All-Soul, while the individual human soul is in contact with that Divine Soul in all its phases, although in varying degrees, according to the measure of its contact with matter. Again we can say what we have already said, that Plotinus knows of no separation between God and his creation.

## The Immortality of the Soul

Greek thinkers believed in the immortality of the human soul long before they succeeded in accounting for their belief on philosophical grounds. Windelband points out that the conception of the body as a prison for the soul, personal immortality, punishment and reward after death, and the transmigration of souls, are all beliefs that can be found even in thinkers like Heraclitus, Parmenides and Empedocles. These beliefs could clearly not have been the product of their systems, for the reason that their cosmogony had a materialistic basis.

But the belief in the immortality of the soul never progressed beyond the concept of a vague semi-material existence as a shade in the lower world, where the external form of the dead human beings is to a certain extent retained. And always it seemed as if that continued existence was dreaded more than desired. Nor could the Olympian cults offer any satisfactory form of immortality to its devotees. It was a subject left to the mercies of popular religious trends. Socrates, to give one example, was sceptical not of the doctrine, but of its utility.

In Plato we do find a definite theory based on his metaphysics. He postulates the pre-existence and immortality of the human soul. The sin for which we are punished here, refers to a previous life,[190] and the lot of the soul hereafter will depend on our conduct now.[191] But even Plato is vague and uncertain. He gives us the impression that the soul will live in eternal contemplation of the ideas, but he fails to tell us what the relation between the soul and the ideas will be. Inge points that Plato is very self-contradictory in this respect.[192] In the *Phaedo*, immortality is accepted, in the *Apology* he is agnostic, while in the *Meno* he is sceptical. Personally, I believe that Plato in a measure accepted the Dionysic doctrine of the transmigration of souls in an endless series of reincarnated existences.[193]

Aristotle apparently believed that soul-kind survived, but he does not accept the doctrine of personal immortality. He also rejects the Platonic conception of reincarnation. The Stoics do not, like the Epicureans, openly deny the possibility of a future life, but the soul to them is in a sense material, and on the whole they are agnostics in this respect.[194]

The Jewish and Christian views on the matter probably had less influence on Plotinus than we might have expected, if indeed it is possible to speak of a Christian view at this stage. The Fathers had no common standpoint. Tertullian regards the soul as material. *Nihil est nisi corpus*, is his definition of it. And a material soul would hardly be immortal. The problem of the Christian interpretation of πνεῦμα is too wide in its scope for this work. A comparison between the Pauline and Stoic standpoints would be instructive. The crux of the problem is, of course, the question whether and in how far the Pauline πνεῦμα was a material concept. It is of importance to know that Origen openly denied the resurrection of the body.[195]

The philosophical heritage in this respect was therefore not of much help to Plotinus, and the only philosopher to whom he is indebted in his proposed solution of this question is Aristotle.

The basis of Plotinian argument in this respect, is the continuity of the divine World and the human soul, and the timelessness of creation.[196] These two theses presuppose one another—an entity created in time must perish in time, and could have no unbroken continuity with the eternal God. And if there is that continuity, one must perforce accept the eternal pre-existence of the human soul. The soul is immaterial, one with God, and 'what reasonable person could then doubt the immortality of so valuable an entity?'[197] This doctrine of continuity is essentially Neo-Platonistic. Porphyry says that the essence of soul is union with God.

But what is this immortality? Does it involve the continued existence of the individual soul? In other words, is the human being individually immortal? Did Socrates pre-exist? And does Socrates, as Socrates, exist now?

There is one passage in the *Enneads* where Plotinus apparently answers this question in the affirmative. He says: 'Thus far we have offered the considerations appropriate to those asking for demonstration. Those whose need is conviction by evidence of the more material order are best met from the abundant records relevant to the subject: there are also the oracles of the gods ordering the appeasing of wronged souls and the honouring of the dead as still sentient. A practice common to all mankind. And again, not a few souls, once among men, have continued to serve them after quitting the body, and by revelation, practically helpful, make clear, as well, that the other souls, too, have not ceased to be'.[198]

It is very important that this passage should be seen in its right perspective. It stands at the end of the tractate in which Plotinus deals with the problem of the immortality of the soul, and he there deals with it in his usual logical way. His conclusions differ materially from the tolerant concessions which he makes in this passage to popular belief. As he says in the opening sentence of the cited passage, he addresses it to those who are capable of logical arguments. Without denying the value of the passage, therefore, I believe I am correct in attaching more weight to the logical sequence of his reasoning, which I shall attempt to follow.

We have already, in a previous section of this chapter, seen that ✓ the human soul is a tripartite entity. There is the lowest, or vegetative phase, the reasonable or specifically human phase, and the divine or intuitive phase. We have also seen these three phases are not separate, since they have their origin in the same source. But the ways by which they emerge from that divine source, are different. The vegetative soul is simply a manifestation of the All-Soul or lower phase of the Soul as hypostasis of the divine Triad. That this vegetative phase of the soul continues to exist after the death of the body, is certain, but Plotinus leaves us in no doubt that it has nothing

further to do with the individual. The All-Soul with its manifestations is merely the expression of the creative power that produced
the visible universe, and it is only found in conjunction with the
embodied world. Plotinus says: 'How is it that when the higher
soul withdraws, there is no further trace of the vegetative principle?
For a brief space there is . . . hair and nails still grow on the dead.
There are signs of a life force still indwelling . . . But is there a
simultaneous withdrawal or frank obliteration? . . . How could it
pass out of being, a thing that once has been? . . . May we not think
that, similarly, the light belonging to bodies that have been dissolved remains in being while the solid total made up of all that is
characteristic, disappears?'[199]

This is clear enough. The vegetative phase of the human soul
reverts to the general manifestation of the All-Soul. It does not
disappear, neither is it accepted as an indispensable concomitant of
the higher phase of the soul. It simply becomes the vegetative
power in some other entity. It is immortal, but because it clings
not to the individual, but to the body, it has nothing to do with
the immortality of the human being. It is a concomitant of bodily
entities as a manifestation of the life of God which creates immanently in the universe, and consequently it can have no bond with
the soul freed from its body.[200] The soul, after death, has no vegetative phase.

But there are two higher phases—the rational and the intuitive.
Can the rational phase survive the death of the body? This question
is extremely important from the personal point of view, because
the rational phase of the soul, as Plotinus saw it, is psychologically
and theologically the soul as we know it. The vegetative soul is
merely the principle of bodily life and growth, while the intuitive
phase is practically one with God. It has no thought, feeling or
memory. It is merely the God in us through Whom we know God.
If it should appear that this second phase of the human soul either
dies or loses its essential functions, we would be entitled to amend
the general consensus of opinion that Plotinus regards the soul as
immortal, and our justified conclusion would be that Plotinus
rejects absolutely the notion of personal immortality. To put it
differently—if the rational phase of the soul does not, after death,
retain its distinctive character, soul-kind may be immortal, but
Socrates is not. The *ego* would cease to exist.

In IV. 4, Plotinus points out that the essential function of the soul when it is freed from the body is intellection or contemplation. Such intellection is timeless. Because there is no past or future in the Ideal World, there is no room for memory. Nor would the soul, in its timeless contemplation of God, have any recollection of the time-space sphere. 'When we seize anything in the direct intellectual act there is room for nothing else than to know and to contemplate the object; and in the knowing there is not included previous knowledge; all such assertion of stage and progress belongs to the lower and is a sign of the altered; this means that, once purely in the Intellectual, no one of us can have any memory of our experience here. Further, if all intellection is timeless—as appears from the fact that the Intellectual beings are of eternity, not of time—there can be no memory in the intellectual world, not merely none of earthly things but none whatever. All is presence there; for nothing passes away. There is no change from old to new'.[201]

In other words, it is not as if death simply terminates all memory of human life and a new memory era is born. All memory is annulled, and because there is no time in the Ideal World and all is an eternal moment, there is no possibility of remembering things that happen there.

From the human standpoint, that could hardly be called immortality. It is clear that the personality, as we understand it, ceases to be. Simply viewed from the common-sense angle, one would be inclined to say that the continuity of experience as expressed in the continuity of memory of those experiences, is an essential aspect of personality. The Soul would live for ever, but the *ego* would cease to exist. Socrates would no longer be Socrates, because the Socrates that lives there, would not even be conscious of the fact that there is an earth or that a Socrates ever existed on that earth.

Plotinus proceeds to make assurance double sure. 'There will not even be memory of the personality, no thought that the contemplater is the self—Socrates for example—or that it is Intellect or Soul. In this connection it should be borne in mind that, in contemplative vision, especially when it is vivid, we are not at the time aware of our own personality; we are in possession of ourselves, but the activity is towards the object of vision with which the thinker becomes identified'.[202]

It is here the case of the drop of water that, after all its wanderings, returns to its source, the ocean. The drop ceases to exist as an individual drop. It is immersed in the ocean. It becomes that ocean.

In the same way the Soul, in its absolute contemplation of God, becomes God. It is no longer conscious of its own individual existence. It has indeed not ceased to exist, but its existence has been raised to a higher order. The drop has become an ocean, the Soul has become a God. 'Once pure in the Intellectual, it too possesses that same unchangeableness: for it possesses identity of essence. When it is in that region it must of necessity enter into oneness with the Intellectual Principle by the sheer fact of its self-orientation, for by that intention all interval disappears. The soul advances and is taken into unison, and in that association becomes one with the Intellectual Principle'.[302]

Had we been able to state that the soul in the Ideal World is conscious of its unity with God, we would have been entitled to attribute some measure of retained individuality to it. But even that much Plotinus is not prepared to grant. The possession of God by the soul is a matter of which the soul is not conscious, but that, according to Plotinus, would merely increase the intimate nature of the relation between them. 'There is such a thing as possessing more powerfully without consciousness than in full knowledge'.[204]

I believe that the above passages adduce sufficient evidence that there is no room for personal immortality in the system of Plotinus. The human soul in the Ideal World shows no similarity whatever with the second or reasonable phase of the human soul on earth. It naturally follows from the words of the philosopher that there can be no perception or discursive reasoning in the case of the soul after death, because these things have to do with external data or stimuli, and no such data or stimuli are possible where all things have become 'one simultaneous existence with God'.[205] With safety we can say that the reasonable phase of the human soul does not exist there. All that remains, is the essential soul, the intuitive phase.

What, then, becomes of the reasonable phase when the body dies? Does it die also? If even the vegetative soul cannot be destroyed, it follows that neither can the reasonable soul. In a later portion of this chapter we will see that the reasonable phase of the human soul can exist only in conjunction with a body. When the body perishes, the soul still exists, but in a pure form. And in that pure form, thought and the other functions of the discursive phase of the human soul cannot find a place.

Why? We have already seen that memory would be impossible.

But why would thought, perception and the other functions cease to exist? Because these functions are the peculiar attributes of the soul in its limitations by the body. The reality of the soul depends on the nature of the work entrusted to it.[206]

And Plotinus correctly regards the functions of the soul in its relation to the body as less exalted because in each of these functions there is imperfection.

'Consider sense-knowledge: its objects seem most patently certified, yet the doubt returns whether the apparent reality may not lie in the states of the percipient rather than in the material before him; the decision demands intelligence or reasoning. Besides, even granting that what the senses grasp is really contained in the objects, none the less what is thus known by the senses is an image; sense can never grasp the thing itself; this remains for ever outside'.[207] And in another tractate he says: 'Knowledge in the reasoning soul is on the one side concerned with objects of sense, though indeed this can scarcely be called knowledge, and is better indicated as opinion or surface-knowing'.[208]

In contrast to this there is the Intellectual Principle whose knowledge is pure self-knowledge, without any sensual perception. And, as we have already seen, the soul, after its release from the body, becomes one with the Intellectual Principle and shares in the attributes of that divine being.

Plotinus nowhere says so in explicit terms, but I believe that the rational and intuitive phases of the human soul are identical, with this reservation: that the former is the soul in its subservience to the body, the latter the soul in its liberty. This is probably what Plotinus means when he says that the intuitive phase of the soul is present in every individual, although very few use it or are even conscious of it. 'The secondary or tertiary souls of which we hear, must be understood in the sense of closer or remoter position. It is much as in ourselves the relation to the Supreme is not identical from soul to soul. Some of us are capable of becoming uniate, others of striving and almost attaining, while a third rank is much less apt. It is a matter of the degree or powers of the soul by which our expression is determined'.[209]

We must therefore conclude that after death the rational phase of the soul, because it is no longer in any relation with a body, must become free or intuitive, released from the necessity of sensual perception.

There are other problems in connection with personal immortality on which Plotinus gives us his views, and the most important of these are metempsychosis and punishment and reward. Inge in his introduction[210] to the few pages that he devotes to this subject, gives a summary of the doctrine of transmigration as found in Oriental religions, and he also points out that Empedocles, who follows Pythagoras in this matter, says that the cause of transmigration is sin, and that the period involved is thirty thousand years.

Plotinus devotes considerable space to this matter, but I am inclined to agree with Inge[211] who thinks that Plotinus did not regard the matter in a very serious light. My own conclusion is that there are very definitely certain passages in the *Enneads* that grant the possibility of παλιγγενεσία, but I disagree with Inge to the extent that I do not believe that those passages are the views of Plotinus himself.

Speaking of providence, Plotinus says: 'We must not forget the well-known words that there is more to think of than the present'. And then he proceeds to enlarge on the 'well-known words'. We read that stupid people become plants, dreamers awake in the next world to find themselves high-flying birds, and unsuccessful politicians come back to earth to continue their work in the appropriate form of bumble-bees. There is no doubt that Plotinus is speaking with his tongue in his cheek when he says these words.

There are other passages which Inge does not discuss. In the first place, as we have already seen,[212] Plotinus very clearly says that the proper function of the soul after the death of the body is the uninterrupted contemplation of the Ideal World. But will that be the lot of all souls? The system of Plotinus gives us no option but to conclude that the answer to this question is in the affirmative. In III. 4, 6 there is an apparently contradictory answer, but it is quite clear that Plotinus is here not giving his own view,[213] but the view of Plato.[214]

We know, of course, that Plato toyed with the doctrines of rebirth and remembrance, and also that he regarded the two theories as mutually inclusive. Plotinus, on the other hand, not only refused to accept remembrance on the part of the soul of the life before bodily death, but he even denies the possibility of any remembrance whatsoever in the Ideal World. It is very clear that he does not accept the Platonic theory of remembrance. Had Plotinus viewed the doctrine of rebirth with any favour, he would at least have attempted to disprove the mutual inclusion of the two doctrines. I believe that I am justified in saying that the passages where rebirth is apparently accepted by Plotinus, either refer to popular belief or the theories of other philosophers.

It is a different matter when we speak of the question of the pre-existence of souls. The Plotinian view in this respect is that the soul, as a simultaneous existent with God, is uncreated. The Ideal World is its natural home, and while it exists in that sphere, it is busied only with its essential task, the contemplation of God. But after its descent into the body, thought begins, with all the varied experience of human life. This descent of the soul is understood by Plotinus to be a gradual one. At first it is in the Ideal World; in other words, it is one with God. In its descent to the human body, there is then apparently an intermediate stage, which he calls the celestial sphere [οὐρανός], but he is clearly at a loss to explain the nature of this condition. A superficial perusal of the tractate concerned (IV. 4, 5–7) conveys the impression that a particular soul becomes dislodged in the Ideal World and descends to the celestial sphere where one of the celestial bodies serve as its habitation. In a previous chapter I have already warned against a literal interpretation of these dicta, based on our connotation of 'soul'. The stars are not 'ensouled' in the sense that the rational or human phase of the soul is present in them, but all things, stars and planets and plants and even lifeless objects like stones, are 'ensouled' in the sense that the 'life' or 'form' of God is immanent in them, in varying degrees. Any entity is real in the degree in which this ψυχή, or 'life', of God is active in that entity. It would be dangerous, if not impossible, to give a detailed gradation of all known entities. Plotinus gives us no systematic axiological scale, and where he does, in part, do so, we need not accept his gradation even though we accept the fact of the relation between the reality of any entity and the degree of immanence in that entity of the 'life' of God.

In his explanation of the descent of the soul from God to the human body he does, indeed, express an opinion on this gradation, and it is to be regretted that he did so. In IV. 4, 5 it is clearly stated that souls in their descent from God, first inhabit the stars.

In other words, one could say, the stars have souls—souls more perfect and nearer to God than the human soul. Yes, such is the view of Plotinus, with this proviso, that we must not interpret 'soul' as the rational phase of the human soul. In other words, Plotinus does not say that stars think, feel, remember, hope and fear, like human beings. What he means is that God is immanent in the stars and in the unity of their movements. The stars, in their existence and in their actions, give proof that God made them, or, to put it differently, that they are an expression of the all-pervading, creative life of God.

Up to this point there is no difficulty in agreeing with Plotinus. We need not agree with him when he states that the degree in which the life of God is immanent in the celestial bodies is higher than the degree in which that life is immanent in the human soul.

That Plotinus does not attribute human souls to the stars, is proved by the following passages from the tractate concerned: 'The question touches memory in the stars in general, and also in the sun and moon . . . if immune from all lack, they neither seek nor doubt, and never learn, nothing being absent at any time from their knowledge—what reasonings, what processes of rational investigation, can take place in them, what acts of understanding? In other words, they have seen God and do not remember (even that)? No. It is that they see God still and always and as long as they see, they cannot tell themselves they have had the vision. Such remembrance is for the souls that have lost it. But can they not tell themselves that yesterday, or last year, they moved round the earth, that they lived yesterday or at any given moment in their lives? Their living is eternal, and eternity is an unchanging unity. The movement of the celestial beings is one movement. It is our measuring that presents us with many movements, and with distinct days, determined by intervening nights. There is all one day; series has no place; no yesterday, no last year'.[215]

Our conclusions in connection with the question of the immortality of the soul, are then the following:

(1) The human soul belongs to the soul-kind of which the soul, as third hypostasis of the Divine Triad, is the source. It is therefore, like all manifestations of soul, immortal.

(2) After the death of the body the human soul again becomes one with the Ideal World.

(3) The human personality is dissolved with death. The condition of the soul in the Ideal World is impersonal, without thought, consciousness or remembrance. It is wholly engrossed in the contemplation of God.

(4) There is no evidence whatsoever to justify the conclusion that Plotinus believed in reincarnation.

(5) Souls are immortal after death, and consequently they were eternally pre-existent before birth.

It is interesting to compare the results of Plotinian thought with the conclusions reached by other Greek philosophers. He differs from Plato who postulated the immortality and pre-existence not only of the soul, but also of the human personality. With Empedocles Plotinus has in common the view that the soul eventually becomes God.

Christian eschatological dogma is in a state of continual flux, and during the first three centuries of the Christian era there was little question of unanimity, even if we should leave out of consideration acknowledged heretics on this point, like Tertullian and Origen. The resurrection of the body would, to Plotinus, have been an obnoxious dogma, but there is not much difference between the standpoint of Plotinus and the Pauline dictum that the visible things pass away, but that the invisible are eternal. And there is a definite Neo-Platonic ring in the words of the same apostle that a certain man was exalted to the seventh heaven where he heard unspeakable words that may not be spoken by a human tongue. That could, perhaps, have been Paul's way of saying that human words, based on the functions of the discursive phase of the human soul, are inappropriate to express the nature of the contemplation of God in the Ideal World. I say, perhaps.

## The Functions of the Human Soul

I shall discuss these functions under the heads of Growth, Sensation, Pain and Pleasure, Memory, Reason and Epistemology. It must be clearly understood that we are now dealing with the specifically human soul and especially with the two lower phases of that soul. The functions of the intuitive or divine phase of the human soul will be discussed in another chapter where our subject will be the nature of the practical religious implications of the system of Plotinus.

## Growth

Plotinus finds the lowest manifestation of soul-kind in the vegetative phase of the human soul. Inge[216] is definitely wrong where he identifies this vegetative phase with the world of plants. He says that the world of plants is the lowest manifestation of the soul. The vegetative soul of the plant is identical with the vegetative soul in man—it is simply the principle of growth. It is, as we have seen, a manifestation of the All-Soul or lower phase of the third divine hypostasis. It is even found in entities where there is otherwise no trace of soul. 'For a short while after death the hair and nails of the body still grow'.[217]

We must not, however, forget that Plotinus finds a manifestation of soul where the vegetative principle need not necessarily be present. Every existing entity is a combination of soul and matter. Matter is the negation of all being, and pure matter does not 'exist'. The bare fact of existence is an indication of the presence of soul in the entity concerned. In this sense, then, 'existence' could be called the lowest and primary manifestation of soul. Apart from any activity of the human soul, the bare existence of the body, even without the principle of growth, is a manifestation of soul. But we could hardly call it a manifestation or function of the human soul. Even the principle of growth is not a specifically human function. Our real field of search will be the discursive phase of the human soul. The vegetative phase belongs to the territory of physiology just as the functions of the intuitive phase is a problem for the student of religious mysticism.

## Sensation[218]

Perception is a function of the living combination—the 'soul-as-using-body' of Plotinus. Neither Soul nor body can have alone perception of any kind. Perception points to external data. The pure soul is one simultaneous existence with the Intellectual Principle, and the 'thought' of that Principle is purely self-thought, arrived at by immediate contemplation, without the aid of perception of external data or the discursive analysis and synthesis of those data. Pure soul would therefore be unaffected by external stimuli, while pure body would be incapable of being so affected. 'A first principle is that the knowing of sensible objects is an act of the soul, or of the living conjoint, becoming aware of the quality of certain corporeal entities, and appropriating the ideas present in them. This apprehension must belong either to the soul isolated, self-acting, or to soul in conjunction with some other entity. Isolated, self-acting, how is it possible? Self-acting, it has knowledge of its own content, and this is not perception but intellection'.[219]

Plotinus, therefore, concludes that bodily organs are necessary for perception, and such organs must lie midway between the object perceived and the soul—the two spheres of sense and the intellectual —without being identical with either. It is akin to the external object by its power of being affected, and to the knower, by the fact that the modification it takes, becomes an idea.[220]

Of the teleological aspect of perception, Plotinus says that sensation is aimed at utility. The object of sensation is a potential source of danger, but by perception we are enabled to deal with it before it can actually do harm. Most types of bodily pains (birth-pains are an exception) tend, according to medical opinion, in the same direction, and pain would thus be a necessary adjunct to the instinct of self-preservation. Plotinus simply extends this view to include all perception.

I have no great quarrel with this standpoint, but it is certainly not in accord with Plotinus' explanation of the relation between action and vision. In a previous chapter we have already seen that he regards actions as weakened vision, and we could deduce from this that sensation would stand in the same relation to intellection (or the perfect self-knowledge of the Intellectual Principle), as action to vision.

In the same tractate Plotinus also discusses the physiological basis of perception. The whole body is illuminated by the soul, and every organ and member of that body shares in the soul in its peculiar way. In this way every function has its own organ through which the soul acts, with the exception of the function of feeling. Here the whole body is an instrument of the soul.

Plotinus is quite modern in his view that the nervous system is the carrier of the motor impulses from the brain to the different parts of the body.[221] But he does not recognize the brain as the author of the other functions like sight, hearing, etc. These organs are to him independent authors, while the omnipresent soul serves as the co-ordinating principle. He says: 'The brain therefore has been considered as the centre and seat of the principle which determines feeling and impulse and the entire act of the organism as a living thing. Where the instruments are found to be linked, there the operating faculty is assumed to be situated. But it would be wiser to say only that there is situated the first activity of the operating faculty: the power to be exercised by the operator—in keeping with the particular instrument—must be considered as concentrated at the point at which the instrument is to be first applied'.[222]

We must, however, not conclude that Plotinus regards the different types of perception as unconnected. They are the sensations of a living being, and consequently there is a mutual bond. This bond is the discursive phase of the soul. There can be no pure sensation. Even the simplest form of sensation presupposes a judgment.

Plotinus does not deal at length with the different organs separately, but he does give a very clear account of his views on sight. *Mutatis mutandis*, his conclusions on this point would also be applicable to other organs.

His first question is whether sight is possible without an intervening medium, like air or a transparent object. His answer is in the affirmative, 'Such an intervening material may be a favouring circumstance, but essentially it adds nothing to seeing power. Dense bodies, such as clay, actually prevent sight. The less material the intervening substance is, the more clearly we see. The intervening substance, then, is a hindrance, or, if not that, at least not a help'.[22]

Vision, or rather sight, is therefore not a case of a progressive handing-on of the object of sight from space-unity to space unity. It is more a case of sympathy. If the organ of vision corresponds to the object of vision, there is an immediate contact. Plotinus cites[224] the case of the fisherman who receives certain impulses from the fish through the rod, although such impulses totally differ in rod and fisherman. Had he lived to-day he would have mentioned the operation of radio, electricity, telephony, and other inventions, where the sympathetic receiving apparatus 'perceives' the power in a different and more efficient way than the wire or the space-wave which serves as the medium.

We often find in the *Enneads* the contention that perception of any kind depends upon the mutual sympathy of the universe by virtue of which all parts are inter-connected, and he is here on idealistically correct ground. The universe can be traced to the One, and because of that common source, all entitites are interlinked. In the same tractate he raises the interesting question whether we would have been able to distinguish entities on another universe, if it were possible for such another universe to exist. He merely asks the question without answering it, but the answer is implicated in his system. Without the common source and the mutual sympathy, perception would be impossible.

*Memory*

We have already seen that Plotinus rejects the possibility of memory in the soul after its release from the body, and consequently it must, to a certain extent, be connected with the discursive soul, in other words, an attribute of the soul-body conjoint. In IV. 6, Plotinus lays down the thesis that perceptions are not impressions, and that memory would consequently not be the passive conservation of perceptions. The soul is not the passive receiver of these things. It is an active agent.

In every perception there is a judgment. Between the pure deed of perception and the accompanying judgment there is a distinction, but no separation. Such distinction is noticed in the case of judgments without preliminary perception, e.g., in the case of judgments touching the Ideal World where perception would be impossible. But although there can be judgments without perceptions the converse is not the case. Every perception is accompanied by a judgment. 'But if perception does not go by impression, what is the process? The mind affirms something not contained within it. This is precisely the characteristic of a power—not to accept impression but, within its allotted space, to act'.[226] The judgments of the soul touching the Intellectual sphere would, of course, not presuppose perception, because 'they come foward from within, unlike the sense objects known as from without'.[227]

The soul, therefore, has contact with the higher and the lower spheres. The former it knows immediately, the latter mediately. 'The Soul is the creative Logos of the universe, the last among the Intellectual Beings, but the first creative Logos of the entire realm of sense. Thus it has dealings with both orders'.[228] To say that the soul *has knowledge* of those higher spheres, would mean that those spheres are subject to analysis, an impossibility in the case of that perfect unity. The knowledge of God that we have, differs from our knowledge of the sense-word, because the former knowledge was obtained intuitively, by virtue of essential uniformity, since the human soul is 'one simultaneous existence' with God. There need be no external data obtained by sense-perception, as a necessary preliminary to such knowledge of God. Plotinus says: 'Of the Intellectuals it is said to have intuition by memory upon approach, for it knows them by a certain natural identity with them; . . . they are its natural vision'.[229]

Our memory of God is therefore in reality no memory. It is merely the recognition of the divine source of the highest in us. It is the intuitive recognition of ourselves. The sublime implications of this Plotinian concept are clear. The dogma of the essential corruption of the human soul finds no place here. Man is not only the highest being in the material universe. He is a part of God. The activity of human thought, desire and whatever else there may be in him, are nothing less than the lapping of the water against the rocks, of which the source is the eternal movement of the mighty ocean, God. For the moment he may be bound to matter and to a body; his glory may be temporarily dimmed, but he is nevertheless heir to eternity.

The moral influence of such a dogma on a tired humanity, waging a hopeless battle against lower forces to which it is bound, can be very powerful. God is, then, no longer a far-off dim Being who can be approached only by the act of mercy on His part, but a reality in every human being, even the most depraved, so that without flinching we may identify Him with the highest in us, and instead of yielding in despair, man would seek that highest in himself. Man would seek his true self, and find God.

But, notwithstanding his divinity, man is also intimately bound to a body, to the sense-world. Here, there is no possibility of memory through identity. The act by which the soul has memory of God, is its essential act. But in the case of external entities it is different. The activity of the soul by which the memory of God is experienced is in this case weakened, because the object is without. 'To the sense-order it stands in a similar nearness and to such things it gives a radiance out of its own store, and, as it were, elaborates them to visibility The power is always ripe and, so to say, in travail towards them, so that, whenever it puts out its strength in the direction of what has once been present in it, it sees that object as present still; and the more intent its effort the more durable is the presence'.[230]

It follows, therefore, that memory is not a permanent presence in the soul. Perception is not an impression and consequently memory is not a reference to such impressions. The fact that by exercising memory it is improved, is a proof of the fact that it is an activity that can become more efficient, and not a reference to an impression that must necessarily be static. For that reason, he says, we sometimes forget, and by applying the activity more energetically, we ultimately remember. Furthermore, if memory were a reference to a static impression stored in the brain, it would become progressively more difficult to remember as more and more things are so stored. But in practice the opposite is the case. 'Those who have learnt many things . . . reach the stage where they can easily remember. We must, therefore, accept the fact that the basis of memory is an activity of the soul which, by practice, becomes more efficient'.[231]

Two further arguments that he adduces in the same tractate against the impression theory are, firstly, that weaker minds would then more easily remember and that the soul would then have magnitude and consequently be a material entity.

The way in which this activity or $\dot{\epsilon}\nu\dot{\epsilon}\rho\gamma\epsilon\iota\alpha$ works, and what exactly happens when the human being remembers, is explained in a previous tractate of the same *Ennead*.[232] In the first place he points out that memory must necessarily deal with a past. It therefore presupposes an agent who is subject to experience in time. God can therefore have no memory. We have already seen that even the so-called memory of the highest phase of the human soul which we call the organ by which we know God, is in reality no memory. Here Plotinus says: 'For the same reason memory, in the generally accepted meaning of that word, cannot be ascribed to the soul in connection with the ideas that are inherent in its essence. It contains those ideas not as a memory, but as a possession'.[233]

Following Aristotle, Plotinus draws a clean line of demarcation between $\dot{\alpha}\nu\dot{\alpha}\mu\nu\eta\sigma\iota\varsigma$ and $\mu\nu\dot{\eta}\mu\eta$. The former is the intuitive memory by eternal possession, the latter is the ordinary human remembrance of things that have taken place in time.

The failure of Inge[234] to explain this matter is no doubt due to his failure to distinguish between the different phases of the human soul. For some reason or other Inge wishes to suggest that the soul is a passive recipient of memory, something which Plotinus, as we have seen, clearly denies. The solitary proof which Inge adduces are the words of Plotinus that $\mu\nu\dot{\eta}\mu\eta$ is a $\pi\dot{\alpha}\theta\eta\mu\alpha$ $\tau\hat{\eta}\varsigma$ $\psi\nu\chi\hat{\eta}\varsigma$.[235]

But neither in that passage nor anywhere else does Plotinus suggest that the soul is a passive recipient. The passage concerned deals with the question whether memory belongs to soul or body. The question whether the agent is active or passive, is not discussed. Correctly, I believe, Ficinus translates it:[236] 'Memoria igitur ad animam pertinet'. An even better rendering would be: 'Memoria igitur est habitus animae'. In other words, the accent falls not on πάθημα but on ψυχῆς.

After determining the difference between μνήμη and ἀνάμνησις in iv. 3, 25, Plotinus proceeds to inquire in which of the constituents of our nature memory is to be found—if in the soul, in which phase of the soul, and if in the body as used by the soul, in other words, in the living conjoint, in what way it is present.[237]

His answer is that perception can only take place in the double nature of body and soul, but that the body is always passive: the soul, active. Consequently the memory of that perception is the task of the soul. There are, for instance, memories of the results of logical reasoning, and that is the task of the soul.[238] Memory is, therefore, as we have already seen from the passage incorrectly cited by Inge, a *habitus* of the soul.

But which phase? Plotinus gives an indirect answer to this question. The intuitive phase of the soul, as divine essence, is a simplex, and consequently not divided into faculties. The vegetative phase may have faculties, but certainly not the faculties of perception, memory, or desire. Memory must therefore be a *habitus* of the discursive faculty of the soul.

Memory is an inevitable result of the condition of the soul in its relation to the world of time and space. We have already pointed out that memory does not take place by identification, but there is to a degree identification between the soul and the objects of its memory. We have seen that memory is an activity, not a passive reception of impressions made on the soul by sensations. But if it comes from the soul as an active agent, there must be a degree of uniformity between the soul and the objects of its memory. Here we touch the centre of the Plotinian system. All things are referred to one common cause and consequently all things are related to one another. By virtue of that relationship, memory is possible. Were it possible to postulate another universe apart from our own, a universe derived from another cause, there would, according to Plotinus, be no perception or memory on our part of the entities in that other universe. That, at least, is the logical implication of his theory that memory presupposes a degree of identity between subject and object.[239]

Finally, I must point out that the relationship between μνήμη and ἀνάμνησις is the same as the relationship between action and vision.

## Pain and Pleasure

Plotinus discusses this question in connection with the problem of the relationship between the body and the soul, and quite correctly he assumes that the body, apart from the soul in it, is ensouled by virtue of the fact of its existence. We have already spoken of the Plotinian theory of the ensoulment of all existing entities and we need not, at this stage, enlarge on it. The body, like all other entities of the sense-world, is matter that, by the action of soul, has received form and attributes. But the ensoulment of the body goes no further than its possession of form, and consequently pain and pleasure cannot be the attributes of the body alone. And in the same way soul, in its unmixed state, is exempt.

But there is an intimate relationship between the soul and the body. Two entities, differing in rank and nature, together form one temporary unity, and as a result of their common natural incapability of forming such a unity, pain is born.[240] Up to this point I have no quarrel with Plotinus, but his further treatment of this subject is in direct opposition to the above theory. In IV. 4, 19 he says that 'pain is the perception of a body bereaved of soul, while pleasure is the recognition of a living body, in which the image of soul is brought back in harmony with the body'. But if pain is the result of the forced unity of body and soul, how can pleasure be found in the intenseness of that unity? If the first thesis is correct, one would expect to find pain in the condition where the unnatural harmony of soul and body is at its peak.

My second objection to Plotinus in this respect is that he totally ignores the pains and pleasures of the body as such. If pleasure were nothing more than the joy of a triumphant soul, animal pleasures would be hateful to the ordinary human being. And yet we are faced by the fact that animal pleasures, even where the soul objects, are also pleasurable, although the enjoyment is in this case of a lower grade than in the case of psychical pleasure.

I believe that Plotinus' failure in this respect is due to the fact that he did not recognize degrees of pain and pleasure. The soul has three phases, and each of those phases has its own pain and pleasure. The body and the soul form a unity, but it is a pseudo-unity, with antagonistic elements, and the victory of the one would of necessity mean the defeat of the other. I cannot agree with Inge where he says that Plotinus correctly regards pain and pleasure as states of consciousness.[241] Plotinus' first thesis is, in my opinion, the correct one, namely that pain is born of the incapability of the soul and the body of forming a unity. But he should not have stopped there. In the association of the soul with the body a pseudo-unity is formed, in which different strata are clearly distinguishable. The soul as power of growth is then the vegetative phase, the soul in its employment of the human organs like perception, etc., is the discursive phase, while the intuitive phase remains unmixed. These three phases differ in the degree in which they are one with the body. The vegetative phase is in the lowest sphere, while the intuitive phase is wholly unmixed. As a result of their varying relationships to the body, they strive after different values, and in the struggle which ensues as a result of the clash of values, pain is born, while pleasure would then be found in the harmonious co-operation of the three phases in the choice of values to be attained.

## Desire

In his treatment of the related subject of desire, Plotinus is more explicit. He clearly says that he is speaking of bodily desires.[242] And he is correct in his statement that the source of desire is the living conjoint of body and soul. The body as such would have nothing to strive for. But Plotinus recognizes two separate phases in any particular instance of desire. In the first place there is the vague unconscious need in the body, and then the transfer of that need to the soul as a conscious desire. The soul would then act as a censor—not all needs would be allowed to become conscious desires. 'From the moment of the sensation the soul, which alone is competent, acts upon it, sometimes procuring, sometimes on the contrary resisting, taking control and paying heed neither to that which originated the desire nor to that which subsequently entertained it'.[243]

Plotinus asks the question why there should be two separate subjects in desire, and why the body, as living conjoint, could not be the only subject. His answer is that, apart from the soul, there are actually two separate entities in the human being, namely the body as body and the body as an ensouled entity. The body is the creature of the soul and is dependent on it. For that reason the body, as body, cannot control the desires of the body as an ensouled entity, and even the ensouled body can do little more than state the need. The soul is the only judge. 'The living body may be said to desire of its own motion in a fore-desiring with, perhaps, purpose as well. But the granting or withholding belongs to another again, the higher soul'.[244] There is therefore a difference between impulse and desire. The former is merely the preliminary to desire. The soul is always at liberty to refuse its sanction, in which case the matter goes no further.[245]

*Reason and Epistemology*

Caird[246] believes that Plotinus follows the intuitionist theory in his espistemology, which Leighton describes as follows: 'The essentials of the intuitionist theory are these: I have immediate or direct acquaintance with external reality in my sense-perceptions. I have immediate or direct acquaintance with internal reality, that is, with the processes of mind, by introspection or the inner sense'.[247]

But this interpretation of Plotinus rests on a misunderstanding of the Plotinian concept of intuition. We have already spoken of the Plotinian distinction between πράττειν and θεωρεῖν. *Mutatis mutandis*, the same distinction is applicable in the case of knowledge and intuition. Plotinus regards knowledge as the result of the imperfect human method of analysis and synthesis, while intuition is the perfection of self-knowledge, when there is complete identity between the subject and object of such knowledge. Such self-knowledge is only possible in the case of a simplex, because even the knowledge that one part has of the other, would not be self-knowledge, notwithstanding the fact that the subject and object may be parts of the same entity.[248]

But that does not mean that Plotinus denies the objective value of knowledge. His standpoint is that in every act of knowing there are two different factors. There is in the first place the external entity that serves as the object of perception. The data so obtained are then classified by the reason. Perception and classification are thus the first steps towards the acquisition of knowledge. 'Sense sees a man and transmits the impression to the understanding. What does the understanding say? It has nothing to say as yet. It accepts and waits'.[249] The second stage is that of the judgment passed by the reason on the data obtained. He says: 'If it should go on to develop the impression received, it distinguishes various elements in what the representative faculty has set before it. Supposing it to say: 'Socrates, if the man is good', then, while it

has spoken upon information from the senses, its total pronouncement is its own. It contains within it a standard of good'.[250]

This, then, is the metaphysical basis of knowledge. The subject
is the human being, and he has in himself a standard derived from the
Ideal World. And that standard is not only connected with the
moral sphere. It is also active in the sphere of truth and of beauty.
There is a kinship between the human soul on the one hand, and the
Absolute Good, the Absolute Beauty and the Absolute Truth, on
the other. And by virtue of that kinship recognition takes place and
knowledge is possible. Such knowledge is only possible because the
Ideal World and the human soul are not separated from one
another. Truth would then be nothing else than the Universal in
the external data, recognized by the universal element in man.

This is very definitely not an application of the Intuitionist theory.
There is more correspondence with the Coherence theory of modern
objective idealists.[251] Joachim[252] says: 'The ideal of knowledge is a
system, not of truths, but of truth'. That one truth is the Ideal World,
the Intellectual Principle, and it is only because that Being is present
in us and in our experience that we are enabled, even by the long
and tortuous method of analysis and synthesis, to arrive at the truth.
The universe is the derivation of a unity, and that unity is immanent
in all existing entities. Truth would then be the correspondence
with that unity, or, to put the matter more simply, the degree of
reality of any entity would depend on the degree in which that
entity participates in that unity. Here we have another point of
contact with the Coherence Theory. No truth can be absolute,
because no entity participates absolutely in that unity. Leighton
says that no truth is absolutely true in itself. According to him, the
degree of truth pertaining to any particular judgment is determined
by the systematic inclusion, in that judgment, of other subservient
truths.[253] Plotinus would have added that this systematic inclusion
is essential because every entity in the universe participates to a
degree in the Intellectual Principle.

This theory is very clearly expounded by Plotinus in his rejection
of the sophistic subjectivism as a basis for the determination of truth.
He says: 'Consider sense-knowledge: its objects seem most patently
certified, yet the doubt returns whether the apparent reality may not
lie in the states of the percipient rather than in the material before
him; the decision demands intelligence or reasoning. Besides, even
granting that what the senses grasp is really contained in the objects,

none the less what is thus known by the senses is an image; sense can never grasp the thing itself; this remains for ever outside'.[254] And truth, for Plotinus, can never be anything outside. It must always be perfect self-identity. It may never allege anything outside of itself. There must be perfect identity between knower and known.[255]

The only Being that satisfies these conditions is the Intellectual Being, where the knower as νοῦς and the known as νοητά form one perfect unity, notwithstanding the logical distinction between the two. Objective truth is the counterpart of the di-unity of the Intellectual Principle. For that reason, says Plotinus, we cannot submit the Intellectual Principle to criticism, because it is truth itself, and truth cannot be criticized, because there is no higher criterion by which it can be tested. Nothing, he says, can be more true than the truth.[256]

From this thesis there flows logically the supposition that something is true only in so far as it corresponds to the Truth, that is, the Intellectual Principle. The possibility of the existence of objective truth is therefore an infallible indication that the Intellectual Principle exists. The same thought is expressed in other words in another tractate,[257] where he says that no entity can possess reality unless there is a simplex independent of that entity. Without such a simplex, the universe would be an aggregate of things that have no being, no reality. The universe, in other words, would be non-existent. The very existence of the universe is a proof that there is an all-embracing unity.

We have seen that objective truth is only possible because the Intellectual Principle is a di-unity. But Plotinus makes it very clear that objective truth is not the *product* of the Intellectual Principle. It is that Principle. In other words, the νοητά are not caused by the thought of the νοῦς. They are that νοῦς. The Intellectual Principle is the truth, and an entity is true in the measure to which it contains that Principle. That Principle is the criterion, and it is present in the human being. The Intellectual Principle is not a thing among things. Consequently we can only find it in its different manifestations, of which the highest is man. Is this the sophistic standpoint that man is the measure of all things, of what is, that it is, and of what is not, that it is not? No, definitely not. On the contrary, this is perfect objectivism that finds the criterion not in man as man, but in man as the highest manifestation of God.

But what, then, of the differences between man and man? Plotinus does not answer this question, although the answer is implicit in his system. The Intellectual Principle is manifested in man in a fuller degree than in other entities, but not in a complete degree. The content of the Intellectual Principle—and even that is an understatement—is the universe. It is the all-embracing archetype of the universe, the cosmic Idea. Truth is the correspondence with the Intellectual Principle, and the Intellectual Principle is the true archetypal cosmos. This is indeed an application of the Coherence theory of truth. For, if truth is the archetypal cosmos, it follows that the individual thesis is true only to the extent in which it corresponds with the cosmos as a whole, and by implication, with all the other individual theses of that cosmos.

Superficially it may seem that this view of Plotinus is very vulnerable. It may be said that even a coherent system need not necessarily correspond to the objective reality, because its basis may be a false supposition. In the case of religious devotees we sometimes find a very coherent system to explain life after death, but apart from the brain of that devotee that system need have no reality. One could conceivably conjure a zoo from one's own imagination.

But in the case of Plotinus this criticism would be faulty, for the simple reason that he does not, like the devotee, ignore certain aspects of reality. There is also coherence with our experience. Before any theory involving coherence can be of value, it must show that our experience has a trustworthy contact with reality. Is this the case with the theory of Plotinus? The objects of our experience have, for him, reality, because they are in contact with the Ideal World. The fact that an entity exists, is already a proof that it has that contact. Viewed from the opposite side, it would mean that the ultimate reality is immanent in all existing entities, not only therefore, in the known, but also in the knower, with the result that there is a dynamic relation between knower and known. Both are factors in the one universe, and they affect one another. In this respect I believe that Plotinus is in advance of idealists before his time. Plato did not succeed in explaining the relation between the objects of our experience and reality clearly, and for that reason his system did not yield a convincing theory of knowledge.

### Is the Soul a Fallen Entity?

Before closing this chapter, the question remains to be answered whether the soul is a fallen entity, in other words, whether the human soul can sin, and if so, whether it has actually sinned and as a consequence has come into disfavour with the higher beings. The problem to be solved is not in the first place an ethical one, but metaphysical. It touches the relation between the soul and God.

We have already pointed out that the human soul is one simultaneous existence with God, and as such it was not unfaithful to its divine source by expending its creative faculties on matter. In his tractate on beauty, Plotinus argues that because every human being has in him, to a lesser or greater extent, the faculty of recognizing beauty, it follows that beauty must be inherently present in every human being. 'Withdraw into yourself and look. And if you do not find yourself beautiful yet, act as does the creator of a statue that is to be made beautiful: he cuts away here, he smooths there, he makes this line lighter, this other purer, until a lovely face has grown upon his work. So do you also . . . until you shall see the perfect goodness established in the stainless shrine'.[258]

In other words, goodness and beauty are inherent in the soul, and although Plotinus realizes that a soul may be 'filled with injustice and desires, torn by internal strife, full of the fears of its own cowardice and the jealousy of its meanness, busied in its thoughts with the perishable and the low, the friend of vile pleasure, living a life of submission to bodily desires',[259] he refuses to grant that these deformities are inherent in the soul. In the same tractate he proceeds as follows: 'What must we think but that this shame is something that has gathered about the soul, some foreign bane outraging it, soiling it, so that, encumbered with all manner of turpitude, it has no longer a clean activity or a clean sensation, but commands only a life smouldering dully under the crust of evil'.[260]

There are, then, souls filled with evil, but that evil is not inherent in the soul. It is a 'crust of evil', and by a process, not of essential rebirth, but of baring the soul to bring to light its essential goodness, the soul is reinstated. The Plotinian theory in this respect shows certain well-marked differences and agreements with the accepted Christian standpoint. The picture painted in the *Enneads* of the soul in its state of evil, may well have been taken from the writings of St. Paul, where the apostle gives the same lurid account of the fallen soul of man. But there is one fundamental difference. According to the Christian standpoint the soul is basically evil. It is helpless, and were it not for the gracious condescension of God, it would be powerless to reform itself. Sin is not a crust; it has become the essence. 'Unless a man be born again' is the *conditio sine qua non* of redemption.

But, according to Plotinus, the soul is not basically evil. The sin is a crust, and by 'cutting away here, smoothing there', the soul, that essentially has retained its divine character, again emerges in the splendour dimmed only temporarily by the crust of material adhesions. This is stated very clearly by Plotinus where, in the same tractate, he proceeds as follows: 'A soul becomes ugly by something foisted upon it, by sinking itself into the alien, by a fall, a descent into body, into matter . . . Let it but be cleared of the desires that come by its too intimate converse with the body, emancipated from all the passions, purged of all that embodiment has thrust upon it, withdrawn, a solitary, to itself again, in that moment the ugliness that comes only from the alien, is stripped away'.[261]

# V

# THE PROBLEM OF EVIL

*What is Matter?*

IN *Ennead* III. 6 Plotinus discusses the question of the immutability of the unembodied. Here we find two extremes. At the top of the scale is the Ideal World, with its three hypostases. The human soul also belongs to that world, and is therefore not susceptible to change. Virtue and vice in the soul are nothing more than harmony and its lack, respectively. There can therefore be no question of any other entity forcing its way into the soul and causing any change in its essence.[262] We have already seen the application of this theory of the immutability of the soul, in our treatment of the question whether the soul is a fallen entity.

But we have spoken of two extremes. Matter is the base of the pyramid, as the Ideal World is its apex. Matter is unembodied and immutable. It is very important to have a clear understanding of the Plotinian concept *matter*. In the tractate concerned, Plotinus describes it as follows: 'Matter must be bodiless, for body is a later production, a compound made by matter in conjunction with some other entity. Thus it is included among incorporeal things in the sense that body is something that is neither Real-Being nor matter. Matter is not Soul; it is not Intellect, is not Life, is no Ideal Principle, no Logos; it is not limit nor bound, for it is mere indetermination. It is not power, for what does it produce? It lives on the farther side of all these categories and so has no title to the name of Being. It will be more plausibly called a non-being, and this in the sense not of movement (away from Being) or station (in non-Being), but of veritable non-Being, so that it is no more than the image and phantasm of mass, a bare aspiration towards substantial existence. It is stationary, but not in the sense of having position; it is in itself invisible, eluding all effort to observe, present where no one can look, unseen for all our gazing, ceaselessly presenting contraries in the things based upon it; it is large and small, more and less, deficient and excessive; a phantasm unabiding and yet unable to withdraw, so absolute is its lack of all being'.[263]

From this passage it is clear that matter is for Plotinus something immaterial and intangible. He regards it as the absolute lack of being, in other words, the imaginary negative extreme to absolute being, that is the Ideal World. He calls it non-being [τὸ μὴ ὄν], and as such it is less than mere lack of existence or being. It is the negation of all possibility of being. For that reason he says that when we call it non-being, it must not be understood merely in the sense of movement away from being, but that it is non-being absolute. It is the logical abstraction of the principle of non-reality. What God is at the top of the scale, that is matter at the base.

In the same tractate Plotinus proceeds to prove that matter is not susceptible to change. There is nothing into which it can change. Nevertheless he asks the question whether it is not possible for matter to accept attributes and be changed by those attributes. His answer is that there are different ways in which some entity can be present in another entity. In the case of bodies the presence of a second entity causes a change, but 'there is also a presence which acts, for good or for ill, with no modification of the object, as we have indicated in the case of soul'.[264] And such is the case with matter. Plotinus here uses the simile of the mirror. He says: 'Mirrors and transparent objects, even more, offer a close parallel; they are quite unaffected by what is seen in or through them. Material things are reflections, and the matter on which they appear is further from being affected than is a mirror. Heat and cold are present in matter, but the matter itself suffers no change of temperature'.[265]

Furthermore, change can only take place in subsidiary things, not in essentials. Should an essential change take place, the entity essentially ceases to exist. Non-being and the lack of all attributes are the essence of matter. Any change would therefore cause an attribute, and that would essentially change the nature of matter. 'If there is to be matter at all, it must be always identically as it has been from the beginning. To speak of matter as changing is to speak of it as not being matter'.[266]

If the essential poverty of matter were a secondary attribute, change would have been possible. 'If it is base in the sense of being Baseness the Absolute, it could never participate in order, and if evil in the sense of being Evil the Absolute, it could never participate in good'.[267] And since matter is the opposite of the Absolute Good, it follows that it must be Absolute Evil.

But notwithstanding this essential poverty of matter, Plotinus gives it a large share in the creative process of which the visible

universe is the product. It is the basis and universal mother of all
becoming. But because it is the basis of becoming, it must itself be
something other than becoming. And even then it must not be
understood in the sense that matter gives becoming to the visible
universe or its entities. The Logos, or the immanent phase of the
Ideal World, acts on matter, and then, in the fashion of a mirror,
by a pseudo-conception of a pseudo-entity, it conceives. Should the
Logos disappear, the visible reflection or created entity would automatically disappear also. For Plotinus the visible universe is merely
the visible reflection of an invisible Reality on a pseudo-reflector.
'Is this (the visible universe) then a pseudo-entry into a pseudo-
entity, something merely brought near, as faces enter the mirror,
there to remain just as long as the people look into it? Yes: if we
eliminated the Authentic Existents from this sphere, nothing of all
now seen in sense would appear one moment longer. Here the
mirror itself is seen, for it has some degree of Real Being. But bare
matter, which is no Idea, is not a visible thing. If it were, it would
have been visible in its own character before anything else appeared
on it'.[268]

On the strength of the cited passages, I believe that we are entitled
at this stage, to come to the following preliminary conclusions:

(1) Plotinian matter is not matter as we know the concept.
It is invisible, without attributes, and without being.

(2) Matter is uncreated, because all creation takes place through
the action of Idea on matter.

(3) Matter does not exist. It is the logical abstraction of Negation-
Absolute. It is the Eternal Nothing.

(4) Because it is the Eternal Nothing, it can never become
anything. It is therefore not susceptible to change.

(5) The visible universe stands midway between matter and the
Ideal World. It is the product of the pseudo-conception caused by
the action of the Ideal World on matter.

Two further statements must be made before we proceed with
the treatment of the implications of these negative attributes of
matter. In the first place it has no mass. The mass or weight of
material entities is a quality, and as such it is derived from the
creative Logos. 'The mass produced by the Idea is, let us suppose, a
man or a horse; the horse-magnitude came upon matter when a
horse was produced on it; when the horse ceases to exist upon the
matter, the magnitude of the horse departs also . . . In bodies,

necessarily compounds, Magnitude—though not a determined Magnitude—must be present as one of the constituents; it is implied in the very notion of body; but matter—not a body—excludes even undetermined magnitude'.[269] The same is true of any other quality. Every quality is latently present in the Intellectual Principle, and only in the visible universe does it come to actuality. Just as colour comes from the colourless prototype of colour in the Intellectual Principle, so size and mass come from the sizeless and massless prototype of those qualities in the Intellectual Principle. Matter is absolutely indefinite and undefined. It is actually nothing, it is potentially everything. For that reason it takes on any form which the Intellectual Principle bestows on it.[270]

In *Ennead* I. 8, the only tractate that served Schröder as a source, Plotinus enquires after the origin of evil and its nature. His first problem is his well-known thesis that knowledge can come only through correspondence, and that there is nothing essentially in the human being that corresponds with evil. 'In what faculty could we possibly know evil? All knowing comes by likeness. The Intellectual Principle and the Soul, being Ideal Forms, would know Ideal Forms and would have a natural tendency towards them; but who could imagine evil to be an Ideal Form, seeing that it manifests itself as the very absence of Good?'[271] At this stage Plotinus leaves this question unanswered. Apparently he argues that an act of knowing includes its opposites, so that we cannot know the Good without being aware of its opposite. In any case, in the next paragraph he proceeds to determine the nature of the Good.

What is the Good? It is, he says, that on which all things rest, towards which all existences aspire as to their source and their need, while itself is without need, sufficient to itself, aspiring to no other, the measure and term of all, giving out from itself the Intellectual Principle and Existence and Soul and Life and all Intellective Act.[272] Clearly he is speaking of the highest phase of the divine Trinity, and he proceeds to point out that in the Ideal World there is no room for evil.

But if there is no room for evil in the Ideal World, which is true being, evil must necessarily fall under the category of non-being, in other words 'that it must be some *habitus* of non-being or that it must be related to non-being in some way'. There would, however, be this proviso: by non-being we must not understand simply a lack of being, but the negation of it, in other words, something of a totally different nature.

From this point onwards Plotinus is on safe ground. His argument is as follows: over against the good in the visible universe, there is the Good-Absolute, namely God. Actually we cannot call God good, because there would be the danger that goodness may be attributed to Him as a secondary addendum. He is not good: He is the Absolute Good. In the same way there is the Absolute Evil over against evil things, where evil is simply an attribute, while in the case of the Absolute Evil it is the essence. 'Does not measure exist apart from unmeasured things? Precisely as there is measure apart from anything measured, so there is 'unmeasure apart from the unmeasured... There must, then, be some Indetermination-Absolute, some Absolute Formlessness; all the qualities cited as characterizing the Nature of Evil must be summed under an Absolute Evil; and every evil thing outside of this must either contain this Absolute by saturation, or have taken the character of evil and become a cause of evil by consecration to this Absolute. What will this be? That Kind whose place is below all the patterns, forms, shapes, measurements and limits, that which has no trace of good by any title of its own, but takes order and grace from some principle outside itself, a mere image as regards Absolute Being, but the Authentic Essence of Evil—in so far as Evil can have Absolute Being. In such a kind, reason recognizes the Primal Evil, Evil Absolute'.[273]

The explanation of this passage is as follows. Let us think of the All as an axiological scale, of which we will call the two extremes the summit and the base. The summit is Absolute Reality, that which has being in the fullest and most perfect sense, namely God, whom Plotinus calls the Ideal World. It is absolute being or reality. It does not exist in the sense that we are able to localize it— it is a logical postulate. We know that God is. Were that not so, we would not have been able to explain the existence of the universe. Let us now grant that the highest degree of reality is also the highest degree of good. Then that summit is at the same time the highest good.

At the other end of the scale is the base—the opposite in every respect of the summit. For Absolute Being we have here Absolute Non-Being, Non-Reality. Like the summit, however, the base is also a logical postulate. And when we here speak of non-being,

I

Plotinus does not wish to denote merely the *non esse*, but the *non posse esse*. All possibility of being is here excluded. And if goodness is to be determined by the degree of reality and being, then we will find at the base of the scale, the Absolute Non-Good, or Evil Absolute. And this logical postulate of the axiological scale, is matter. It does, of course, not exist. How can the principle of absolute non-being have existence? And if it does not exist, if it has no reality, it demands no creator. That answers the old question as to how and why God made the devil. Evil, according to this view, is simply the absence of reality. An entity is good according to the measure in which the summit of which we have spoken is present in that entity, and evil is measured in the converse way.

But the very fact that the ultimate reality, or, as we have called it here, the summit of the scale, is present to a varying degree in all entities, is a proof of the fact that it is also absent to a varying degree from all entities. Consequently every entity is good to a certain extent and evil to a converse extent. Evil is then simply the degree in which a given entity is still subject to matter. In other words, it is a necessary stage of development in the history of the visible universe.

Actually there is no entity that does not to a certain extent participate in the ultimate reality, just as there is no entity that participates fully. Let us, as a logical postulate, imagine an entity so low in the scale of participation, that it is absolutely deprived of God. That non-existent base is Plotinian Matter.

In this connection there is a very important question to be answered. What of the evil soul? Plotinus clearly says that the embodied entity is evil to the extent in which it participates in matter.[274] But the soul is not essentially in any relation to matter. Its union with the body is a temporary condition, and it is not of the essence of soul. If it were, the soul would cease to be, after the bond between body and soul has been severed by death. And yet we know by experience that there are evil souls, and that every soul is, to a certain extent, tainted by it. Plotinus attempts to answer this question in *Ennead* I. 8, 4, where he says: 'But what is the root of this evil state? How can it be brought under the causing principle indicated? Firstly, such a soul is not apart from matter, is not purely itself. That is to say, it is touched by unmeasure, it is shut out from the forming Idea that orders and brings to measure, and this because it is merged into a body made of matter. Then if the reasoning faculty, too, has taken hurt, the soul's seeing is baulked by the passions and by the darkening that matter brings to it, by its decline into matter, by its very attention no longer to essence but to process— whose principle or source is, again, matter, the kind so evil as to saturate with its own depravity even that which is not in it but merely looks towards it. For it is wholly without part in Good, the negation of Good, unmingled lack'.[275]

In other words, two factors are here in operation. In the first place, there is the fact that the soul is bound to a body and that body is bound to matter. There is, consequently, an open road for matter to influence the soul. The very fact of its association with body causes an inevitable lack. In the natural course of events essence is abandoned for process. Intuition becomes analytical reasoning, vision becomes action. Only the intuitive phase of the soul remains pure, and as we have seen, Plotinus tells us that although all men have that phase, few use it. The discursive or essentially human phase of the soul is, to a large extent, under the influence of the body, and consequently subject to matter. I have already spoken of the fact that intuition is abandoned for reasoning. In the Ideal World there is no seeking after knowledge. In its contemplation of the Ultimate Reality the soul is one simultaneous existence with the Ideal World. But in the sphere of space and time the soul is deprived of that immediate knowledge, and it is forced to combat its ignorance by the painful and uncertain way of discursive reasoning. In the same way different desires are born as a direct result of our association with the body. In point of fact, all desires have their origin there. The self-sufficiency of the Ideal World knows no desires because there is no lack.

But the association of the soul with the body is not the only important factor. Plotinus makes it quite clear that, in that association with the body, the soul, of its own choice, becomes more deeply involved in matter than the natural association with body necessitates. Moral evil, according to Plotinus, is not the natural association with the body, with its concomitant lack, but the unnecessary yielding to the influence of matter. He says: 'Evil is not in any and every lack; it is in absolute lack. What falls in some degree short of the Good is not evil; considered in its own kind it might even be perfect. But where there is utter dearth, there we have Essential Evil, void of all share in Good . . . Mere lack brings merely not-goodness. Evil demands the absolute lack'.[276]

This is really the crux of the problem, namely the question what entities participate in evil, and in what measure an entity is evil because it is not all good. And it is very clear that Plotinus is not prepared to draw a clear line of demarcation. The principle on which he works is clear enough. We can put it as follows: There is no moral stigma on man because he shares in the common limitations of bodily life. His association with the body is not-good, because it causes a condition of lack. But before there can be a stigma of moral evil, there must be a definite choice of the will to increase that lack.

Now comes the problem. What causes that choice? If it is matter, then every lack must be evil, and not matter. And a second question must be answered, namely, whether there is a possibility of determining in what measure of lack there is evil and in what measure it is merely not-good. Plotinus says 'that any considerable short-coming makes the ultimate fall possible, and is already in itself an evil'.[277] But what is a considerable shortcoming?

The first problem brings us to the question of predestination and the free will. In this case everything will depend on our answer to this question. If man is in any considerable degree predetermined by his nature, or by the will of a higher being, to make a choice of the lower values and to neglect his own true calling, it follows that the moral cause of evil would be in that volition of the higher being, and man immediately becomes a morally neutral entity. Even matter would then be neutral.

Plotinus answers this question in *Ennead* III. 1, where he deals with Fate. He points out that, in connection with the Ideal World, we can speak of determination and causality only in so far as the essence causes the act. God knows only self-causation. But in the case of all other entities there is the causal series.[278] Everything that happens in the sphere of process, and that includes everything except the Ideal World, has a cause. To deny causality in the sphere of process would not be to bring liberty. It would be a determination stronger than the most mechanical causality. Plotinus knows that the All is the universal cause, but 'not to be willing to penetrate deeper indicates a sluggish mind, a dullness to all that calls us towards the primal and transcendent causes'.[279]

He points out, for instance, that causes apparently identical, have different results. What is it that causes two persons to react differently to the same set of circumstances?

We need not here devote too much space to a discussion of the different theories which Plotinus rejects. The Atomic Theory suggests that everything depends on the way in which the constituent atoms of an entity are joined together. 'Such teaching obtrudes this compulsion, an atomic necessity, even upon God'.[280] We have already, in a previous chapter, discussed the possibility that the stars are causes. Another view is that there is a supreme Fate, but he rejects that theory, even though one could regard God as that Fate. The *ego* would then disappear before God, and God would immediately become the cause not only of the good, but also of evil.[281]

Plotinus' positive standpoint is as follows. We have already seen that everything outside of the Ideal World, that is, the world of space and time, is determined. The determination of the Ideal World is merely self-determination, in other words, perfect freedom. There are therefore two separate *genera*, the free and the determined. The human being belongs to both *genera*. He is partially divine and partially bodily-material. Those deeds which we do in obedience to the bodily aspect, are causally determined, while our deeds done in subservience to the true *ego* are divine, and therefore self-determined and free.[282] He says: 'All things and events are foreshown and brought into being by causes; but the causation is of two kinds. There are results originating from the soul, and results due to other causes, those of the environment. In the action of our souls all that is done of their own motion in the light of sound reason of the soul's work, while what is done where they are hindered from their own action, is not so much done as suffered. Unwisdom, then, is not due to the soul, and, in general, if we mean by Fate a compulsion outside ourselves, an act is fated when it is contrary to wisdom. But all our best is of our own doing. Such is our nature if we remain detached. The wise and the good do perform acts; their right action is the expression of their own power. In the others it comes in the breathing spaces when the passions are in abeyance. But it is not that they draw this occasional wisdom from outside themselves; simply, they are for the time being unhindered'.[283]

Let us now go back to the question as to the cause of the evil choice of the human soul. We have the answer in the double nature of man. Man is divine, self-determining, free and good. By virtue of his embodiment he is closely associated with matter, that is evil. And matter is the cause of his wrong choice.

But what of moral responsibility? Surely, if I am forced to do a wrong deed by some external entity, I cannot be held morally responsible. Plotinus answers this question by saying that man is responsible not because he chooses the lower—matter is responsible for that choice—but because he ceases to be himself. In connection with the question as to the degree of lack that constitutes moral guilt, we have seen that Plotinus speaks of 'a considerable lack'. Perhaps we can explain this by saying that an act will only then be morally wrong when the agent neglects to use to the full the power of self-determination that he possesses by virtue of his unity with the Ideal World. I am not responsible for the fact that I am associated with a body, but I would be responsible if I failed to prevent that association, with its concomitant lack, from gaining an undue influence on my life as a result of my failure to make use of my divine liberty which I have by virtue of my unity with the Ideal World. Practically applied, it becomes still clearer. God, who is not associated with a body, does not think as human thought is understood, because human thought is directed towards the acquisition of knowledge, and God knows all things immediately. But I am not so fortunate. Whatever knowledge I gain, I must gain by the painfully slow method of study, by discursive reasoning and by the synthesis of incomplete data. In other words, my act of thought manifests a lack due to my association with body. But it is not morally wrong, even though there be a lack. But if, through laziness or some other avoidable cause, I should neglect to use what brains I have and so unduly increase my ignorance which is a heritage of my association with the body, I should be morally guilty, not because of my ignorance, but because of my failure to use the imperfect measure of self-determination that is my right.

That is what Plotinus means when he says: 'We are not to think of evil as some particular bad thing, injustice, for example, or any other ugly trait, but a principle distinct from any of the particular forms in which, by the addition of certain elements, it becomes manifest'.[284]

But what of things like sickness, poverty and those other ills that are the lot of mankind? Plotinus here distinguishes between general and moral evil,[285] in the same way as in the passage previously cited. But both are caused by the same factor, namely matter, the absolute lack. Moral and general evil are in their nature identical; the moral aspect appears when the human soul yields to matter and ceases to exercise its self-determination. 'Sickness is excess or defect in the body, which, as a material organism, rebels against order and measure; ugliness is but matter not mastered by Ideal-Form; poverty consists in our need and lack of goods made necessary to us by our association with matter, whose very nature is to be one continual want'.[286]

And, what is more, the existence of these things is an external existence, because although particular evil things and vices have only come to light after the appearance of men and things on earth, matter is eternal. 'If all this be true, we cannot be, ourselves, the source of evil; we are not evil in ourselves. Evil was before we came to be; the evil which holds men down, binds them against their will; and for those that have the strength—not found in all men, it is true—there is a deliverance from the evils that have found lodgement in the soul'.[287]

Matter is therefore the absolute evil. Man is in contact with matter only for a time. Man is therefore not essentially evil.

We must, however, guard against the assumption that, because matter is evil, and this universe is material, while the Ideal World is not material, there are therefore two local spheres, and that man should flee to heaven to escape evil. If man is 'true to his own self', he can live on earth after the pattern of the Ideal World. The correct way of escape is not death. 'The flight we read of consists not in quitting earth, but in living our earth-life with justice and piety in the light of philosophy'.[288] It is therefore possible for man, by the aid of his reason, to banish evil from his life.

The question why there is evil on earth, Plotinus answers by saying that it is a cosmic necessity. If there is an absolute good, or God, there must also be that which is removed from it. And if we proceed far enough in the scale of values, we must eventually come to that which is absolutely removed from God—the negation of everything that is God.[289] What is the universe other than the visible product of the progressive mastery of God over matter? If there had been no evil, there would have been no universe, and if one could conceive of a time when all evil shall have disappeared, when the process of mastery shall have been completed, one would have to remember that such a condition would presuppose the end of the visible universe. As long as the embodied remains, there will be entities where evil and good exist side by side.

Such an entity is good because it is the Logos in its action on matter, but it is also evil because it is matter on which the action takes place.

Does Plotinus see any difference between the concepts vice and matter? There is the same distinction as between the concepts God and virtue. The one is the principle of the other. Just as the Idea of colour in the Ideal World itself has no colour, so God, as the Idea of virtue, has no virtue. In the same way there is no vice in matter, which is, in a way of speaking, the 'idea' of vice. Vice is always the attribute of some entity, the result of the association of that entity with matter. But matter is itself no entity. 'The measureless is evil primarily; whatever, either by resemblance or participation, exists in the state of unmeasure, is evil secondarily, by force of its dealing with the Primal—primarily the darkness, secondarily the darkened. Now vice, being an ignorance and a lack of measure in the soul, is secondarily evil, not the essential evil, just as virtue is not the Primal Good, but is likeness to the Good, or participation in it'.[290]

And just as we cannot segregate God or localize Him so that we can say: This is God, or, there He is; so evil remains but a logical postulate. We see it only in the things in which it is present. But those things are not absolute evil, just as the things in which we see God is not God Himself.

But if evil has no place in the essence of soul, how can we know it? We must remember that knowledge implies a certain measure of correspondence. Plotinus answers this question by pointing out that matter and evil are not realities. They are the negation of reality. And because of our unbroken continuity with the Absolute Reality, we are aware of any absence of that Reality in any entity, but of its absolute absence we can have no knowledge. In other words, we cannot know absolute evil, because in such absolute evil there is nothing akin to us. The Absolute Reality has no place in in it. What we see is not evil, but entities participating in evil to a certain extent. For that reason matter must remain to us a logical postulate. We know that there is such a thing, not because we know it or can see it, but because without it we can find no explanation of the evil that we see in those entities of which we have knowledge. 'We see partial wrong; from what is before us, we divine that which is lacking to the entire kind thus indicated; we see that the completed kind would be the indeterminate; by this process we are able to identify and affirm evil'.[291] In other words, just as we cannot see colour apart from the entity on which that colour is imprinted, so we cannot see evil apart from the evil entity.

We have already, in a previous section of this chapter, given a few preliminary conclusions in connection with the nature of evil. We can, I believe, summarize our further findings as follows:

(1) Negation-Absolute stands in direct opposition to God, who is the Absolute Reality.

(2) Evil must be identified with this Negation-Absolute, and it is therefore nothing else than the lack of God or the Good. Evil is not a positive entity. It is simply the absence of the Good.

(3) Nowhere can absolute evil be found. Evil is only found in entities which, by virtue of their existence, participate to some extent in the Good.

(4) We know evil by virtue of our affinity with God, by being aware of the measure in which God, or the Good, is absent from any given entity.

(5) Moral evil differs from absolute evil in the fact that the former is merely one of the forms under which the latter becomes manifest. It includes the guilty neglect on the part of the human being to use and develop to the fullest possible extent, the divine aspect in him. Simple lack of God, caused by our natural participation in body, is evil, but not moral evil.

(6) The measure in which an entity is dominated by matter or evil also implies the measure in which that entity is dominated by the causal series.

(7) To ask for the author of evil is a *petitio principii*, because it presupposes that evil has an author. Lack can have no author. It is the primal condition. It is a cosmic necessity.

(8) Vice and matter are in the same relation to one another as is the case with virtue and God.

At this stage we are in a better position to ask the question: What is the source of evil? Did God make it or did man cause it? Our answer is that nobody made or caused it. Can the absolute negation of all existence and all reality have an author? That which does not exist can surely have no author or creator. Evil is nothing else than the fact that God is present in a varying degree in different entities, and the measure in which He is not present in any entity, is the measure of evil in that entity. Everything that we can see or think is consequently partially evil, because our thoughts and actions have to do with the world of sense, and everything in the world of sense participates in God and in matter, and is therefore partially good and partially evil. The imaginary point where God is not, and where there is therefore an absolute lack of reality, is absolute evil.

Does this mean that Plotinus denies metaphysical evil? No, but he does deny that evil has reality. The absolute lack of reality cannot have reality.

Before we close this chapter on the nature of matter and evil, it would be instructive to see what other writers have to say on this subject. I shall take, as representatives of the different theories, the works of Schröder and Caird. Schröder's[292] attempt to solve the problem in a dissertation of sixty-four pages inevitably failed by reason of the fact that his only source was the eighth tractate of the first *Ennead*. The result was that the background of Plotinian philosophy was lacking. There is no short road to the heart of Plotinus. The abstraction of one tractate, and the attempt to deduce from the isolated theses in such a tractate a solution of any of the major problems that occupied the mind of the philosopher, must inevitably lead to confusion. Without embarking on a lengthy discussion of Schröder's work, I shall merely mention the following points where I disagree with his conclusions.

(1) He says that Plotinus attributes metaphysical reality to matter and evil, and he talks of an Idea of the 'nichtseienden' in the Intellectual Principle. The fact is that he never mentions the νοητά, and one wonders how he succeeded in concluding that the absolute negation of all reality could find a place in the νοητά, or how the negation of reality could be one simultaneous existence with the very principle of reality.

(2) According to Schröder, Plotinus regards the embodied as essentially and totally evil (*immer und ganz schlecht*). Schröder never discusses the metaphysical basis of the visible universe, but the fact that he says in his dissertation that matter is a necessity because it acts as the basis of the visible universe—a standpoint with which I am in complete accord—would lead one to expect that he would also have realized that the embodied entities of the visible universe are compounds of matter and idea. The embodied can therefore not be totally evil, because it participates in the Intellectual Principle. Schröder did not realize that the embodied is an intermediate stage between the Absolute Reality and the absolute negation of reality. The one is the absolute good, the other the absolute evil. One need only read the tractate entitled *Against the*

*Gnostics* (*Ennead* II. 9), to realize how highly Plotinus thought of the visible universe.

(3) In his discussion of the distinction between moral and metaphysical evil, Schröder speaks of the three kinds of souls of Plotinus. He does not see three phases of one soul, but three different entities, of which the first is pure, the second partially pure, and the third impure. In the chapter on the Soul I have already dealt with this problem at length.

Edward Caird[293] discusses the theological and ethical questions in connection with Plotinus, without especially touching on the metaphysical problems. He takes as the basis of his discussion the incorrect interpretation that Plotinian matter is an eternal reality and that it forms a dualism with God. On the nature and pseudo-reality of matter Caird is silent. We have already seen that Plotinus attempts to retain the liberty of choice of man as a moral creature. From that, Caird concludes that evil has come into the world as a result of the choice of man. Apart from the fact that this is most definitely not the standpoint of Plotinus, it must be pointed out that had Plotinus regarded man as the author of evil, the problem would not have been solved. If man's choice caused evil, evil must have been inherent in man. But man, as an embodied entity, is partially good and only partially evil and can therefore not be the absolute evil. But Caird's interpretation of Plotinus does not answer this question, and Caird realized that it offered no solution. He states that he fails to see how Plotinus can avoid the conclusion that God placed evil in man. But it is Caird, and not Plotinus, who is at fault. Caird misses the basic thought in Plotinus that evil is the negation, the lack, of reality. And a lack has no author.

Caird goes on to say that even if we were to say that matter is the author of evil, the whole problem would again be referred to God, because 'God also made matter'. But to say that, is to confess a total misunderstanding of Plotinus. How could God have made matter if matter is the negation of all reality and existence? Matter is not created. One cannot say that it 'is', only that it eternally 'is not'. For that reason Plotinus calls it the 'Absolute Lack'. Caird's interpretation is as utterly wrong as the interpretation of Inge where he says that Plotinus holds that matter was created, but not in time.[294] Inge refers to *Ennead* III. 2, 1 but in that tractate Plotinus speaks of the creation of the visible universe. Surely the visible universe and matter are two totally divergent concepts in Plotinus. Matter, according to Plotinus, is uncreated. It could not have been created, because it is nothing else than the negation of the presence of God, the utter lack of Reality, the *non posse esse*. Would God create the negation of all reality and existence and would He bring into being the absolute lack of all being? One possible escape from a dualistic view of the ultimate reality is the Plotinian solution of the unreality of matter and the identification of matter and evil. And then to say that 'Plotinus regarded matter as created, but not in time', is to misunderstand utterly the basic principle of Plotinian philosophy.

Caird believes that Plotinus attempted to evade the dualism by suggesting that God did not of His own volition create matter, but that all creation takes place regardless of the will of God. There are two objections to this view. In the first place, Plotinus makes no suggestion of this kind. On the contrary, he clearly says that it is the nature of the Ideal World to create.[295] Creation did therefore not take place regardless of the will of God. Or did Caird expect to find a discursive argument in the mind of God, where creation as a possible mode of action was weighed and ultimately approved? But surely even a cursory perusal of the *Enneads* would be sufficient to prove that Plotinus does not ascribe discursive reasoning to God, and that that form of reasoning was limited to man, with all his limitations of body and time?

And in the second place, even if it were the case that creation took place regardless of the will of God, would that solve the question? Would we not be forced to seek a *tertium quid* which constrained God to create, regardless of His will? But then that *tertium quid* would be God, and the author of both good and evil. And then the whole question would have to be argued again, and, like Omar Khayyam, we would come out by the same door as in we went.

Perhaps the basic error of Caird and Inge is a wrong interpretation of the concepts of πρᾶξις and θεωρία in Plotinus. God does not will something, because in Him volition and essence are one. For that reason His creatures come to life by θεωρία, and not by πρᾶξις. The latter is the human way, creative action made imperfect by the limitations of space and time. Because God creates by intuitive vision, without a preliminary decision of a discursive mind, we may not say that God creates against His will.

A second solution of the problem that Caird finds in Plotinus is that the world is good, notwithstanding many isolated cases of evil. In other words, Plotinus solves the problem by denying its existence. After our discussion of the problem of evil, I do not think it necessary to adduce proofs from the *Enneads* that Caird is wrong. It is true that Plotinus, in his attack on the pessimism of the Gnostics, in *Ennead* II. 9, defends the visible universe by pointing out that, if we grant that the visible world is but an image of the Intellectual Principle, and not its reality, we must come to the conclusion that it is a good image. We find the same sentiment in *Ennead* III. 2, but throughout he grants the existence of evil.

Caird's difficulty here is, of course, that he misunderstands the Plotinian concept *matter*. He says that 'Plotinus regarded matter as the utmost result of the activity of God'. I would be guilty of repetition if I were to attempt to refute so apparent a misrepresentation of Plotinus. Surely God would not have made the negation of Himself.

And the result of Caird's faulty interpretations is that he finds a hopeless dualism in Plotinus. He is forced either to regard God as good and bad at the same time, or otherwise, in Oriental fashion, to postulate two eternal principles in eternal opposition to one another. And that, according to Caird, is what Plotinus actually does.

Inge, the great English student of Neo-Platonism, is guilty of the same error. We have already discussed his finding that matter was created, although not in time. Apart from the objections already named, I have this further objection to the interpretation of Inge, that he implies that there was any creation whatsoever in time. In our chapter on the Soul we have already pointed out that Plotinus denied all creation in time, and in a later chapter on Time and Eternity we will come to the same conclusion.

I believe that, if I understand Plotinus correctly, the problem of evil is solved by him in a more logical way than any other of the problems dealt with in the *Enneads*. Whether we accept his final conclusions or not, I believe that he has nowhere in the course of his arguments been guilty of illogical reasoning, or the postulation of a dualism.

# VI

# THE ETHICS OF PLOTINUS

## The Metaphysical Basis of Plotinian Ethics

IF Ethics were nothing more than the enumeration of certain rules of conduct, it would have been sufficient to draw up a Plotinian decalogue from the *Enneads*. But before any rule of conduct can be regarded as binding and authoritative, we must know on what metaphysical grounds those rules are based. Before we can believe in a *must*, we must know whether and why there is a *must*, and who or what is the basic principle of that *must*. In the same way the believing Christian accepts the existence and being of God as the basis of the Christian moral code, and that basis immediately becomes the unconscious law-giver, whether by explicit formulation or by implied principles.

But however conclusive a basis may be which rests on religious belief, the philosopher demands something totally different. The aim of philosophy is the consistent application of the results of logical thought. As a Christian, one would acknowledge the absolute authority of the command given by Christ that we must love one another, but the philosopher, and even the Christian philosopher, would go further, and ask why such a command, or any command at that, should be given to us, and what the metaphysical basis is of any moral obligation.

Turner[296] found the philosophic basis of moral obligation in the relation between reality and its time-space constituents. In some instances it is revealed in mechanical necessity, but in the case of man, as moral being, it appears as moral obligation. 'What in the physical world was originally a command, impossible to disregard, now becomes a demand, which may be recognized, or repudiated, by the absolutely free choice of the individual'.[297] In Plotinus I found a practically similar answer to the question.

In *Ennead* v. 5, 5 Plotinus expresses himself as follows: 'The series of beings following upon the First bear, each, some form or idea derived from that source. In number the participation establishes quantity; in the realm of being, the trace of the One establishes reality'. This is perfectly in accord with the system of Plotinus as discussed in the foregoing pages. Every entity, however low in the scale of values, participates in God. We live not in a multiverse, but in a universe. The plurality around us points to a basic unity, of which 'the traces are existence'. All existing entities participate in that unity. We have already come to that conclusion in the case of the epistemology of Plotinus, and it is also true in the case of his axiology. God is the source of truth and reality.

On the other hand Plotinus points out that God is not truth and reality. 'It follows that the First must be without form, and if without form, then it can be no being; Being must have some definition and therefore be limited; but the First cannot be thought of as having definition and limit, for thus it would be not the source but the particular item indicated by the definition assigned to it. If all things belong to the produced, which of them can be thought of as the Supreme? Not included in them, this can be described only as transcending them; but they are Being and beings. It therefore transcends Being'.[298]

The next step in our argument is that for Plotinus truth, reality, and beauty are synonymous in the Ideal World. For that reason he gives different names to God. As the source of all being, the unifying principle of all the existing entities, He is the One. His name is the Beautiful, in His character as the source of all beauty. He is called the Good, because He is the transcendent source of all goodness.

Our problem is now to decide in what way man is under a moral obligation by virtue of the fact that there is such a Being who is the basic principle of all virtue. Plotinus gives no explicit answer to this question. We are therefore constrained to argue on the general principles implied in his system.

We have already seen that there is a continuity between the One and the Ideal World on the one hand, and man and the visible universe on the other. In our discussion of the human soul, this became especially clear in the fact that the intuitive phase of that soul is in immediate contact with God. In other words, God and man meet intimately in the intuitive phase of the human soul. There they are one. Now we know that it is the nature of God to be the source of all existing entities. He is also the source of virtue. And if that is the nature of God, it must also be the nature of man in his most distinctively divine phase. In other words, because God is the source of all virtue, and because God and man are essentially one, man, in his most divine phase, namely the intuitive soul, is also the source or basis of virtue. Man would be false to his own nature, were it otherwise. The metaphysical basis of moral obligation is implicit in man himself. There is no external law-giver who demands blind obedience to a moral law imposed from without. Because of the continuity of God and man, the transcendent source of all virtue is man's own self. Turner, as we have seen, found the basis of moral obligation in the relation between reality and its time-space constituents, in other words, in the continuity of the universe and in the fact that man is a creature of God. There is no essential difference between the two standpoints. In acknowledging the binding nature of moral obligation, man by implication acknowledges the immanence of the eternal in the temporal, the continuity of man and God.

Let us view the matter from another standpoint. Man, together with all that exists, shares in reality and also in matter, that is the negation of reality. Man, as an embodied entity, is therefore real and unreal. But his relation to matter is not essential to his nature. It is a temporary relation, lasting only as long as man is in the body, and while the relationship exists, it limits and thwarts his true nature. As soon as that temporary relationship ceases, matter loses all power over man. The essential man, that is, the divine aspect of man, continues to be. If man is to be true to his own self, he must be true to what is essentially himself, especially since that true self is the measure of reality in him, while the material aspect is his measure of unreality. And where the reality in him is the source of virtue, it automatically becomes the basis of moral obligation. Man is subject to moral laws because God is the transcendent source of those laws, and man is essentially in continuity with God. Obedience to the moral law is obedience to the essential self; and this is not subjectivism, because the essential self is the eternal immanent in the temporal. Obedience to the essential self is merely the recognition of the continuity of God and man, and of the essential unity of the universe. The moral man acts *sub specie aeternitatis* because he is obedient to the eternal principle immanent in him, which is his essential self.

## The Subject of Morality

In our daily experience we come into contact with moral and a-moral beings. Plotinus knows two further categories, namely the super-moral and the sub-moral. The super-moral is the Ideal World. In *Ennead* I. 2, 1 where he discusses the source of morality, he clearly says that, because the One is the source of virtue, it cannot have virtue as an attribute. 'It is from the Supreme that we derive order and distribution and harmony, which are virtues in this sphere; the Existences there, having no need of harmony, order or distribution, have nothing to do with virtue; and, none the less, it is by our possession of virtue that we become like to them. Thus much to show that the principle, that we attain likeness by virtue, in no way involves the existence of virtue in the Supreme'.[299] The same thought is repeatedly found in Plotinus. 'We may not call it the Good, if the Good is to be taken in the sense of some member of the universe; if we mean that which precedes the universe of things, the name may be allowed'.[300]

We see, therefore, that God does not possess virtue. Virtue is that which indicates the immanence of God. He cannot be that which indicates his immanence. He is the norm by which virtue is measured. He can therefore not have virtue as an attribute.

But that does not mean that God is a-moral or immoral. The reason why He is not included in the moral sphere is because He is the source of that sphere, and as such He is super-moral. His relationship to morality is the same as his relationship to knowledge, thought, and those other essentially human functions. He transcends those values.

The sub-moral sphere is the sphere of matter. We have already seen that Plotinus regards matter as the source of evil, as evil-absolute. From the *Enneads* it is clear that matter not only never changes or improves, but is essentially incapable of improvement. The sixth tractate of the third *Ennead* deals with the impassivity of the unembodied, and naturally he includes matter in that concept. 'We may take it, then, that while all the qualities and entities that appear upon matter group to produce each the effect belonging to its nature, yet matter itself remains immune . . . to speak of matter as changing, is to speak of it as not being matter'.[301] In the same tractate he points out that, if matter were in any way subject to change, it would have to receive something by the addition of the new arrival. But if it were to receive anything, it would no longer be matter, because matter is the absolute lack, the absolute negation of all existence.

The subject of virtue must be a changing and changeable being,

K

capable of varying conduct, of improvement and deterioration. Something which is essentially evil, and incapable of anything else, would as little be included in the moral sphere as that being that is absolutely good, and which is incapable of evil choice or deterioration. The one is *non posse non peccare*, the other is *non posse peccare*, and even these terms would not be permissible, because the term *peccare* has a moral connotation. It presupposes a norm, and in the case of God and matter no norm is possible, because the former is the norm of what is good, the latter of what is evil. In the tractate on the origin of evil,[302] Plotinus points out that, *mutatis mutandis*, matter stands in the same relationship to evil as God to virtue. 'The measureless is evil primarily; whatever, either by resemblance or participation, exists in the state of unmeasure, is evil secondarily, by force of its dealing with the primal—primarily, the darkness, secondarily, the darkened. Now vice, being an ignorance and a lack in the soul, is secondary evil, not the essential evil, just as virtue is not the primal Good but is likeness to the Good, or participation in it'.[303]

What, then, is the subject of virtue? It is man, who participates in the super-moral and the sub-moral spheres; in other words, that being who is subject to moral change, because he is at liberty to direct his actions to either of those two spheres.

But man is a composite being. There is soul and body, and the body is akin to both matter and the Ideal World, while the soul has three phases. We have already seen in our discussion of the Soul that it is the standpoint of Plotinus that the soul of man is not a fallen entity, and that it is, furthermore, incapable of falling. 'The soul, then, in us, will in its nature stand apart from all that can cause any of the evils that man does or suffers'.[304]

But how can we absolve the soul of man from vice if we remember that it is in the soul that all human thought and reasoning takes place? We find the answer to this question in the Plotinian description of the soul. It is, as we have seen, a divine entity, in continuity with the Ideal World, the highest manifestation of God, and therefore essentially good. If the soul were to sin, it would be a case of God sinning, and that is patently impossible. That, according to Plotinus, is the essence of sin, that man ignores the soul, and acts in obedience to some other master. 'The Intellectual Principle has held aloof from the act and so is guiltless; or, as we may state it, all depends on whether we ourselves have or have not put ourselves in touch with the Intellectual Realm either in the Intellectual Principle or within ourselves. For it is possible at once to possess and not to use'.[305] The 'Intellectual Principle' of which he speaks here is, of course, the intuitive phase of the soul.

At the same time it is clear that the body cannot be the subject of virtue. Where there is no possibility of discrimination, we cannot speak of morality.

But what remains? If neither soul nor body is the subject of virtue, we must seek an intermediate entity, and Plotinus finds that in the living content of body and soul, as he calls it τὸ ζῶον. The soul has, as we know, three phases: the intuitive or unmixed phase, the discursive phase and the vegetative aspect. The first is divine, the third is purely the principle of growth, in which there is patently no possibility of moral choice. But in the second, or rational phase, we find the living conjoint, the *animal commune*. It is in reality the pure soul in its relation to the body. For that reason it is limited by the necessity of discursive thought as a tortuous method for the acquisition of knowledge.

This rational phase of the soul is man as we know him. It stands in a certain relationship with the Ideal World and matter, and its exact position with relation to those two extremes depends on its own choice. And in the liberty of that choice we find the basis of moral responsibility. 'When we have done evil, it is because we have been worsted by our baser side—for a man is many—by desire or rage or some evil image . . . we have acted at the call of the less worthy'.[306]

Here we have a confirmation of the conclusion reached at the end of the previous section, when we found that there is moral obligation because man must be true to himself, in other words, to his divine nature. Here we see that the aspect of man that makes the choice is the subject of virtue.

## Virtue and the Virtues

We have seen that the subject of virtue is the discursive phase of the human soul, and that it is to a large extent subject to the influence of matter. That entity is at liberty to follow the dictates of its own divine essence, or to yield to the influence of matter. The former choice will lead to virtue, the latter to its opposite. Two questions remain to be answered in this connection. In the first place we must decide what the essence is of a correct choice, and from the nature of

that essence we must deduct the practical virtues and in that way
establish the necessary rules of conduct.

From what has already been said, we will expect that virtue will
consist in the progressive self-purification by the discursive soul
from all the stigmata of matter, with which it is in contact. Plotinus
says: 'The soul's true good is in devotion to the Intellectual Principle,
its kin; evil to the soul lies in its frequenting strangers. There is no
other way for it than to purify itself and so enter into relation with
its own; the new phase begins by a new orientation. After the
purification, then, there is still this orientation to be made? No: by
the purification the true alignment stands accomplished'.[307]

This is the exact opposite of the Christian dogma on this point.
The soul is not essentially evil, nor is it, in the words of the creed,
naturally inclined to hate God. It is an essentially good entity and it
need only be purified from its association with matter to appear
as a divine and perfect entity.

Is purification, then, the essence of virtue, and is virtue a negative
matter? Or is purification nothing more than a necessary preliminary step? Plotinus answers[308] these questions by pointing out
that virtue is more than merely the absence of foreign elements.
Before the arrival of the foreign element, there was goodness, and
that goodness will reappear after the disappearance of the intruding
matter, but the purification by itself will not yet be virtue. It will
not be a negative attribute. Plotinus says that the virtue of the
purified soul will consist in the fact that it will see the Ideal World.
As sight is affected by the thing seen, the soul admits the imprint,
graven upon it and working within it, of the vision it has come to.[309]

This happy condition is not a gift given to the soul by purification.
It was always there, even during the period when the influence of
matter dominated the soul, but the vision was darkened by the
foreign element with which it was in contact. The positive effect
of the purification will be vision, and the fruit of vision will be
identity with the Ideal World. In this connection it is interesting to
note that Greek verbs denoting vision, especially ὁρᾶν and ἰδεῖν, very
often have the meaning of participation. In the New Testament we
read of people who will not *see* death, who will *see* the kingdom of
God, where the meaning is really *to experience* or *to participate in*. We
must understand the soul's vision of the Ideal World in the same
sense.

The question now arises whether the identity of soul and the Ideal

World will put an end to the influence of matter over the soul. Plotinus answers by saying that as long as the soul remains in the body, in other words, as long as the living conjoint, the *animal commune*, shall continue to exist, a certain influence will always be exerted by matter. Things like pain, desire, and passion, and those other affections that hinder the soul, there will always be, but their influence will be diminished to the necessary minimum, and the soul as such will be untouched by them. 'The soul will hold itself above all passions and affections. Necessary pleasures and all the activity of the senses it will employ only for medicament and assuagement lest its work be impeded. Pain it may combat, but failing the cure, it will bear meekly and ease it by refusing to assent to it. All passionate action it will check: the suppression will be complete if that be possible, but at the worst soul will never take fire, but will keep the involuntary and uncontrolled outside its own precincts, and rare and weak at that. The soul has nothing to dread, though no doubt the involuntary has some power here too. Fear must therefore cease, except as far as it is purely monitory. What desire there may be can never be for the vile; even food and drink necessary for restoration will lie outside the soul's attention, and the sexual appetite not less'.[310]

This passage gives a very clear view of Plotinus' attitude. One would not call it asceticism, because he does not forbid the pursuit of pleasure and the avoidance of pain, but he places those matters under the strict control of the soul.[311] I find this breadth of view very strange, if we remember that Porphyry, in his life of Plotinus, very clearly says that the master was ascetic in his own way of life. But whether he was an ascetic or not, there is no doubt that he was broad in his moral precepts.

There is one peculiar aspect of the Plotinian moral code, and that is that it has an extremely individualistic trend. The presence of matter forces the soul to be always on the alert, and the only safe place is the inner sanctum of the soul itself. This is one of the Neo-Platonistic traits that has always been the subject of comment, and often it has been regarded as a proof that the followers of Plotinus were a group of nebulous mystics instead of logical philosophers.

But the accusation is undeserved. The Neo-Platonists were not the first school that preached a morality of the inner soul. Aristotle held the same view, and the Stoics went so far as to recommend suicide as an easy method to banish the world. Plotinus did not go as far as that. On the contrary, in *Ennead* I. 9 he strongly deprecates suicide, and he points out that if the condition in which we leave this world will, to a certain extent, determine our status in the next, there should be no thought of leaving while there is any possibility of improvement. In connection with this individualism we must remember that the era in which Plotinus lived contributed to a large extent to his choice. It was a period of general pessimism, and in his chapter on the third century Inge[312] gives a number of quotations from Christian and pagan authors, wherein the common sentiment is that the world had grown old, and that life in it was no longer worth while. We must also remember that Plotinus saw in the human soul the organ of immediate contact with the Ideal World and reality, and even though the world had been a pleasant place in which to live, it would still have been better to pay attention to that realm where the soul has its true essence.

Nevertheless Plotinus did not unduly stress introspective virtue. In his moral series he grants a place to civic virtues as a preliminary to the highest virtue. Of these civic virtues he has very little to say, and there is no doubt that the nature of the times in which he lived had much to do with his silence. Rome at that time was in a period of decline. Porphyry tells us that Plotinus was given permission by the emperor Gallienus and his wife Salonina to rebuild a city in Campania and to rule the adjacent territory according to the rules and laws of Plato.[313] Porphyry adds that the permission was withdrawn by reason of the jealousy of certain courtiers. The withdrawal of the permission was probably a happy chance, because the realization of the plan would have brought no glory to our philosopher. But it at least shows that Plotinus was not indifferent to civil affairs, and it was his standpoint, as we have seen, that civic virtues were a necessary preliminary to perfect virtue. 'Is it possible to be a proficient, a master in dialectic, without these lower virtues? It would not happen. The lower would spring either before or together with the higher. And it is likely that everyone normally possesses the natural virtues from which, when wisdom steps in, the perfected virtue develops. After the natural virtues, then, wisdom, and so the perfecting of the moral nature'.[314]

In *Ennead* I. 2 Plotinus gives a clear description of the natural or civic virtues, and in that tractate he identifies virtue with the process of attaining likeness to God. There is, he says, naturally no possibility that there can be any civic virtues in the Ideal World, since those virtues can only apply to souls that are in a certain relationship with other men, and no such relationship is possible in the case of the Ideal World. But although these things are not in God, we cannot say that they do not produce likeness to God. He points out that we know by experience how excellent some men can be as a result of their possession of civic virtues. That excellence is also divine. We can, therefore, by the possession of civic virtues, attain some measure of likeness to God. 'It is from the Supreme that we derive order and distribution and harmony, which are virtues in this sphere. The Existences there, having no need of harmony, order or distribution, have nothing to do with virtue; and, none the less, it is by our possession of virtue that we become like to them'.[315]

This passage is perfectly in accord with what the *Enneads* have so far told us. The Ideal World is the source of thought, beauty, and whatever other values there may be in the time-space sphere. But it does not possess those values as attributes. The same is true in the case of virtue.

With reference to the civic virtues, we find that Plotinus adopts the four cardinal virtues of Plato, namely wisdom, courage, temperance and justice.[316] The first is the distinctive virtue of reason, the second of the emotional make-up, the third of the combination of reason and the emotions, and the last refers to the relationship between the different constituent elements of man. These virtues have, of course, only value in this sphere. 'The civic virtues are a principle of order and beauty in us as long as we remain passing our life here'.[317]

These civic virtues are divine, although not in a perfect degree. 'They carry a trace of the highest good in the Supreme'.[318] But he differs from Plato in his standpoint that these virtues only have a place in the world of sense. It is the counterpart of the discursive phase of the soul, and like that phase, it takes an intermediate stand between matter and reality. Only in that position is the discursive phase of the soul possible, and only there are the civic virtues of any avail. In the perfect unity of the Ideal World there is no need for civic virtues. In the absence of the body there will be no passions. Temperance will therefore be unnecessary. There will be no cause for fear, and consequently the need for courage disappears. In that world the discursive phase of the soul is merged in the intuitive soul, because there is no embodiment. Consequently errors of judgment are impossible, and the virtue of wisdom becomes unnecessary. Nor is there any justification for the virtue of justice.

But if these civic virtues, however necessary they may be in this sphere, do not bring likeness to God, there is obviously a need for something more, and the second stage in the moral series Plotinus finds in purification or *katharsis*. Referring to Plato, he says that 'true likeness to God is a flight from this world with its ways and things'.[319] All virtues, barring the civic virtues, are purifications.[320]

The *modus quo* of this purification is as follows: The soul of man is subject to matter by virtue of its association with the body. It follows, therefore, that if there is to be positive virtue, there will, in the first place, have to be a purification, a removal of those things that are the basic cause of vice.[321] Naturally we have here a totally different *genus* of virtue from the civic virtues, because the latter are indebted for their existence and necessity to those very entities that have to be removed or at least disarmed before the positive virtues can make their appearance. It follows that this goal cannot be reached while the body is alive, and the purification can therefore be only partial. It simply means that the soul must liberate itself as much as possible from the influence of those factors that originate from the intimate relations of soul and body of which the product is the *animal commune*. 'As the soul is evil by being interfused with the body, and by coming to share the body's states and to think the body's thoughts, so it would be good, it would be possessed of virtue, if it threw off the body's moods and devoted itself to its own act'.[322]

This katharsis is therefore essentially a moral process. In our treatment of the origin of evil we saw that metaphysical evil becomes moral evil as soon as the natural limitations of man are aggravated by a wilful surrender to those limitations. These natural limitations are, of course, not removed by katharsis, but their power is weakened by the elevation of the soul. It is a case of the uphill road, the crucifixion of the body as preached by the New Testament, the healthy and wholesome asceticism without which virtue is impossible. There is neither in the Plotinian nor in the Christian demand for self-discipline any trace of a denial of the natural life. It has become the fashion among writers to ascribe such a denial to Plotinus and to regard him as a gloomy recluse who was ashamed of his own body. It is true that his biographer tells us that he appeared self-conscious in connection with his body and that, as a result of that feeling, never spoke of his ancestors or place of birth.[323] Inge speaks of the exaggerated 'otherworldliness' of Plotinus, and he says that the philosopher regarded this world as a place from which one must escape as fast as possible.[324]

But I believe that these judgments are not substantiated by the total impression conveyed by the *Enneads*. If one reads the well-known tractate entitled 'Against the Gnostics', one comes to the conclusion that the philosopher was profoundly under the impression of the beauty and the grandeur of the visible universe. Possibly his life was more ascetic than his ethics demanded, but our subject is not the personal character of Plotinus, but the philosophical system contained in the *Enneads*.

The basic principle implied in the idea of katharsis is the essential goodness of the soul. Because it is in continuity with God, it is divine, and consequently essentially and eternally good. Evil may cling to the soul, but it can never be of the soul. Its contact with matter may darken its lustre, but it can never destroy it. Consequently the removal of material adhesions will bring to light the soul in its essential purity and lustre. Plotinus says that 'the purification of the soul is simply to allow it to be alone; it is pure when it keeps no company; when it looks to nothing without itself; when it entertains no alien thoughts'.[325]

This doctrine of the necessity for katharsis is, of course, perfectly in accord with the doctrine of the divine nature of the human soul. Were something more than katharsis needed to render the soul pure and unsullied, the implication would be that there is something essentially in the soul, something, in other words, that would not be removed by purification, causing it to be incapable of true virtue. In that case the soul would have a two-fold origin. Apart from its divine kinship it would be derived from the unknown something which renders it incapable of virtue. But a soul that is in direct continuity with the Ideal World, sprung only from the Supreme, would have in its essential nature nothing that is strange to that source. Virtue would then be simply a return to the natural un-sullied state, not a going forth to seek something as yet foreign to it. Nor would vice be an essential constituent of such a soul, and the liberation from its influence would not involve the acquisition of something new, but merely the removal of what is foreign. The soul would then be like the diamond that is made beautiful not by the addition of a foreign element, but by the removal of those adhesions that dim the native lustre of the gem.

Plotinus does not tell us much of the practical application of this process of purification. In his discussion of the metaphysical basis of beauty he compares the katharsis of the soul with the journey of

Odysseus. It is a return to the fatherland, and in the case of the soul, that fatherland is the Ideal World. The nature of the purification excludes practical directions. Such directions would necessarily deal with external things, and the kindly light leading us through the gloom of space-time limitations is an inner light. 'This is not a journey for the feet; the feet bring us only from land to land; nor need we think of couch or ship to carry us away; all this order of things you must set aside and refuse to see; you must close the eyes and call instead upon another vision which is to be waked within you, a vision, the birthright of all, which few turn to use'.[326] There is no doubt that he is here referring to the intuitive phase of the human soul, which, as we have already seen, is one with the Intellectual Principle.

In the same tractate Plotinus uses a simile which gives some indication of his meaning. He says: 'Act as does the creator of a statue that is to be made beautiful; he cuts away here, he smooths there, he makes this line lighter, this other purer, until a lovely face has grown upon his work; so do you also. Cut away all that is excessive, straighten all that is crooked, bring light to all that is over-cast, labour to make all one glow of beauty and never cease chiselling your statue, until there shall shine out on you from it the godlike splendour of virtue, until you shall see the perfect goodness surely established in the stainless shrine'.[327]

There is no doubt that the purification is as much a deed of metaphysical self-orientation as of morality. The Orphic saint would have told us of a command to abstain from certain articles of food and to avoid the presence of birth or death. But these external matters would have carried no weight with Plotinus. Purification is a discipline of the mind, and contamination takes places only when the mind devotes itself to material things.

Thus far purification. It would have been correct to deal here also with the third and final step in the pilgrimage of the soul, namely the attainment of oneness with the Ideal World. But strictly speaking it is not a question of ethics, and we shall therefore discuss it in a later chapter on the religious mysticism of Plotinus.

In conclusion, I may point out that there is a definite correspondence between the theory of purification as found in the *Enneads* and the teaching of Socrates that knowledge is virtue. In other words, think correctly and purification from the taints of matter will be the result.

# VII

# ON BEAUTY AND ART

Plotinus deals with this problem in two tractates,[328] of which the one is a more practical, the other a more theoretical treatment of the subject. In *Ennead* I. 6 he asks the question what beauty is. It manifests itself, he says, in many diverse forms, affecting different organs and emotions of the human nature. There is, in the first place, the beauty that can be seen, heard or felt; and secondly, the beauty of the soul which we find in a way of life, in action, character, intellectual love and virtue. Plotinus asks the question whether there is 'one principle from which all take their grace, or is there a beauty peculiar to the embodied and another for the bodiless?'[329] And his first step towards the solution of this problem is the inquiry into the essential nature of beauty.

Plotinus cannot accept the theory that beauty is the product of symmetry. Aristotle[330] speaks of the instinctive desire for harmony as one of the causative factors in art, but Plotinus points out that in that case only a composite entity can be beautiful. The different parts will be beautiful not in their own right, but only because they co-operate to form a harmonious whole. But experience teaches us that the beauty of an entity is often in converse relation to its complexity. The simple things of life appeal most strongly to our sense of beauty. And even in the case of complex things that are beautiful, there is sometimes a temporary loss of beauty with a retention of the symmetry. And in the case of abstract things there can be no symmetry, but there can be beauty. And how, he asks, can there be beauty in the Ideal World, since that world is essentially a simplex, and not a composite entity?

His own theory is perfectly in keeping with his philosophical system. All things participate in the Ideal World, and in the measure of that participation we find the measure of its beauty. 'And the soul, by the very truth of its nature, by its affiliation to the noblest existents in the hierarchy of being, when it sees anything of that kin, or any trace of that kinship, thrills with an immediate delight, takes its own to itself, and thus stirs anew to the sense of its nature and of all its affinity'.[331]

We have here a coherence or remembrance theory of beauty. The recognition of beauty is the recognition of the immanence of the eternal in the temporal, and the mutual kinship of all existing entities by virtue of that immanence. It is worthy of mention that our search for beauty leads us along the same road that we followed in the case of our search after goodness and truth. In the ninth tractate of the fifth *Ennead* Plotinus clearly says that God can be reached also by the road of our innate love of beauty. All values converge on God. They are values merely because their presence in the time-space universe points to the immanence of the eternal in the temporal, and also to the transcendence of God, because those values have their basis and source in Him. The aesthetics of Plotinus is based on his metaphysics.

He proceeds to ask the question what the relation is between those entities that have beauty as an attribute, and the Ideal World that is the source of that beauty. 'On what principle does the architect, when he finds the house standing before him correspondent with his inner ideal of a house, pronounce it beautiful? Is it not that the house before him, the stones apart, is the inner idea stamped upon the mass of exterior matter, the indivisible exhibited in diversity?'[332] We call something beautiful when we see something imprinted on it that we recognize as our own, by virtue of our continuity with the Ideal World, and the immanence of that world in the object where we recognize beauty.

But there is also beauty apart from any object of the world of time and space, although there also our awareness of beauty is nothing else than a recognition of the presence of God. 'What do you feel in the presence of the grace you discern in actions, in manners, in sound morality, in all the works and fruits of virtue? And in the beauty of souls? When you see that you yourself are beautiful within, what do you feel? What is this Dionysic exaltation that thrills through your being, this straining upwards of all your soul, this longing to break away from the body and live sunken within the true self? These are no other than the emotions of souls under the spell of love . . . All these noble qualities are to be reverenced and loved, but what entitles them to be called beautiful? . . . Anyone that sees them must admit that they have reality of being, and is not real being, really beautiful?'[333]

In other words, truth and beauty are synonymous concepts. They are manifestations of the same Ideal World which is their common source. The love of the soul for beauty is caused by the Intellectual Principle which is at the same time responsible for the manifestation of beauty and our recognition of it.

If that is beauty, what, then, is ugliness? Inge[334] says that it is wrong *form*, but that, for Plotinus, would have been a contradiction in terms. Form, or the νοητά, is for him the divine element, and there can be no wrong or misplaced divinity. Plotinus describes ugliness as the absence of form, or rather the fact that form is obscured by the influence of that which has no form. When he speaks of the vice or ugliness of the soul, he says: 'What must we think but that all this shame is something that has gathered about the soul, some foreign bane outraging it, soiling it, so that, encumbered with all manner of turpitude, it has no longer a clean activity or a clean sensation, but commands only a life smouldering dully under a crust of evil; that, sunk in manifold death, it no longer sees what a soul should see, may no longer rest in its own being'.[335]

Ugliness of the soul is therefore the invisibility of its form due to the presence of matter. Ugliness and beauty are correlative concepts. The one is the measure of participation in the Ideal World, the other the measure of non-participation. But there is no entity in which that world is totally present or absent, and consequently absolute beauty, like absolute virtue, is as much a logical abstraction as absolute vice or absolute ugliness. The same principle applies here as in the case of the absolute evil and the absolute good, the absolute reality and its absolute negation.

But if beauty is the degree of the participation of any entity in the Ideal World, what, then, is art? According to Plotinus[336] it is the transfer to matter of the conception of beauty on the part of the artist: in other words, the expression in a time-space medium of the recognition of the presence of the Ideal World in a time-space entity; or, in yet other words, the expression of the emotions of the sentient artist when, by virtue of his own continuity with the eternal, he recognizes the immanence of that eternal principle in some time-space entity. He mentions the case of the two blocks of stone. The one block is transformed by the artist and becomes a statue, and by reason of that transformation it assumes beauty. That beauty is not inherent in the matter, but in the form given to it by the artist. The beauty is derived from the soul of the artist. It is the expression in stone of the emotions of the artist, and those emotions have been caused either by the intuitive contemplation of the Ideal

World by the artist, or by the realization of the artist of the immanence of that Ideal World in some time-space entity, in this case probably a human being.

We have here, then, a certain imitation, a μίμησις. But it is not the μίμησις of Aristotle,[337] where the work of art is a copy of a material entity. It is the μίμησις of the immaterial Ideal World, of the νοητά, in the soul of the artist. Aristotle says: 'Since the objects of imitation are men in action, and these men must either be of a higher or a lower type, it follows that we must represent men either as better than in real life or as worse, or as they are'.[338] Art, according to Aristotle, is therefore the imitation of the good or the evil, and above all, it is the imitation of material or semi-material entities. For Plotinus it is the imitation of the immaterial and perfect Ideal World, in a material or semi-material medium. For Aristotle the work of art would be lower than the entity that it represents. I make a statue of Socrates. It is only an imitation of Socrates, and therefore less than Socrates. With Plotinus it is otherwise. The statue of Socrates is not an imitation of the time-space entity that is Socrates, but of the idea of Socrates, the νοητόν of the man, or, in other words, of the manifestation of the Ideal World in the time-space entity Socrates. The work of art is therefore higher than the time-space entity.

Plotinus clearly says that art is not a naked reproduction of the object concerned, but it 'goes back to the Ideas from which nature itself derives, and adds where nature is lacking'.[339]

In the last *Ennead* there is a passage where Plotinus speaks of the relation between beauty as the attribute of beautiful entities, and beauty as the eternal essence of the νοητά of God. The former he calls τὸ καλόν, while God is ἡ καλλονή. The καλλονή in the soul of the artist is therefore the author of the καλόν in the work of art.

Can we speak of the beauty of God? Inge[340] distinguishes between the One and the Intellectual Principle. I have already spoken at length of this erroneous distinction, and without repeating the arguments adduced, I may say that in no passage in the *Enneads* dealing with beauty and its relation to God, is there any indication that Plotinus makes that distinction. The Plotinian standpoint is that nature and art are equal in rank, because both are derived from the one source, namely God. The subject and the object of the perception of beauty are related by their common participation in the Ideal World, and it is by virtue of that kinship that the artist

perceives beauty in the entities around him. 'If you are still unmoved and cannot acknowledge beauty under such conditions, then
looking to your own inner being you will find no beauty to delight
you, and it will be futile in that state to seek the greater vision, for
you will be seeking it through the ugly and the impure'.[341] In other
words, when the essential kinship between the subject and object
of the perception of beauty is obscured by the soul's failure to cul-
tivate its intuitive phase, the work of the artist becomes impossible.
Only the man in contact with God can see and reproduce beauty.

Visible beauty therefore points to the invisible beauty, that is God.
And what is the essence of that eternal beauty? Plotinus calls it
intellection, perfect self-knowledge. But the vision of that beauty
is only for those who are capable of finding God in their own
souls. More than a logical mind is necessary to reach to that beauty.
As in the case of the highest virtue, so with the recognition of the
highest beauty, the agent is the intuitive phase of the soul. There is
no question of looking outwards. The highest manifestation of the
eternal values is in the human soul. We are essentially in possession
of the beauty that is God. Were that not so, we would have been
incapable of recognizing beauty in the time-space entities around us.
That divine principle in us is the soul in its purest and highest form,
the essential man, freed from the impure influence of matter, or the
ugly, or the evil, call it what you will. Knowledge of God is perfect
self-knowledge, and the recognition of beauty is nothing else
than the recognition of the eternal value of the human soul. For that
reason the vision is granted only to them who love beauty by self-
identification, and for them it is not difficult to realize that visible
beauty, although its source is divine, is but a secondary manifestation, and that art is not the imitation of the time-space entity, but
the expression of the soul's joy when it realizes its kinship with all
manifestations of beauty, by virtue of its own participation in the
eternal beauty.

It is worthy of mention that Plotinus always comes back to God.
Whether he deals with ethical or metaphysical problems, or life or
beauty, every road leads to the common source of all those values,
here manifested in different spheres, but one in the Ideal World.
Truth and beauty and goodness and life are one.

# VIII

## ON TIME AND ETERNITY

PLOTINUS assumes axiomatically that eternity must be the proto-type of time, if at least, he says, there is any relationship between the two concepts.[342] But he rejects the view that eternity and the Ideal World are identical, in the first place, because we speak of the Intellectual Principle as being eternal,[343] and that, according to him, cancels the possibility of identification; and secondly, because the view that eternity and the Ideal World are identical concepts would necessarily involve the correlative thesis that time and the visible universe are also identical, a theory that is patently erroneous. I have no objection to the second reason adduced by Plotinus, but his first ground is definitely unacceptable. How can he use as an argument the fact that we ascribe eternity to the Intellectual Principle as an attribute? In our treatment of his discussion on the hypostases of the eternal world we have seen that no attribute can be ascribed to these hypostases, and surely the fact that we, in a manner of speaking, call the Ideal World eternal, is no ground for accepting as a fact that eternity is an attribute of that world. Predication involves complexity, and God must be a simplex.

A second hypothesis is that eternity must be identified with 'rest there', in contrast to 'movement here'. Plotinus soon disposes of this theory. Rest, he says, will then have to be taken either as rest in general, or as rest in the Ideal World. If the first meaning applies, eternity would be nothing more than stagnation, and if the second were true, everything outside the Ideal World would be immediately excluded from eternity.

In his positive arguments he begins by asking what must be included in the concept *eternity*. 'It must be at once something in the nature of a unity and yet a notion compact of diversity, or a kind, a nature, that waits upon the existents of that other world, either associated with them, or known in and upon them, they collectively being this nature which, with all its unity, is yet diverse in power and essence. Considering this multifarious power, we declare it to be essence in its relation to this sphere which is sub-stratum to it; where we see life, we think of it as movement; where all is unvaried identity we call it repose; and we know it as, at once, difference and identity when we recognize that all is unity with variety'.[344]

For the sake of the exegesis of this passage, I refer to our treatment of the categories of the Intellectual Principle, where Plotinus speaks of identity and difference, and rest and movement. The Ideal World is the archetype of the visible universe. In that visible universe, which is but an image, we find a variety of things and values, a pluriformity that, however, points to a transcendent unity. Correctly we seek to find the basis of that unity in the creative or rather contemplative archetype. But that is not sufficient. If nothing more than unity were found in that archetype, we would not have been able to explain the existence of pluriformity in the visible universe. An absolutely monistic archetype would not have been able to produce a universe.

But Plotinus found the principle of unity and of pluriformity in the Intellectual Principle, in its νοῦς and νοητά. And we must remember that the concept *eternity* is inseparably associated with the archetypal cosmos. It therefore follows that unity and pluriformity, or let us call it identity and difference, must necessarily be categories of the concept *eternity*. That is what Plotinus means when, in the passage under discussion, he says that 'with all its unity, it must be diverse in power and essence'. By virtue of that qualification it is the *causa finalis*, the teleological basis, of the visible universe.

Eternity can therefore not simply be an accumulation of particles of time. Eternity cannot be endless time, for although time be endless, it is nevertheless time. Eternity is, as Plotinus says, a 'notion compact of diversity', an eternal moment.[345]

The same can, *mutatis mutandis*, be said of the concepts of rest and movement. Rest, then, coincides with the unity or νοῦς of the Ideal World, while movement would be an aspect of the νοητά, or difference. The conclusion to which Plotinus comes is that eternity is 'the life of the Supreme'.[346] It is the expression of the self-identity of the Ideal World. It knows no past or future. It is an eternally immediate being. 'All its content is in immediate concentration at one point; nothing in it ever knows development; all remains identical within itself, knowing nothing of change, forever in a now, since nothing of it has passed away or will come into being, but what it is now, that it is ever'.[347]

Eternity is therefore the declaration of the self-identity or perfec-

L

tion of the Ideal World. It exhibits an absence of past or future—attributes of an imperfect being. 'That which neither has been nor will be, but simply possesses being; that which enjoys stable existence as neither in process of change nor having ever changed, that is eternity. Thus we come to the definition: the Life instantaneously entire, complete, at no point broken into period or part—which belongs to the Authentic Existent by its very existence—this is the thing we have been probing for, this is eternity'.[348]

It will be remembered that Plotinus denies that eternity could be identified with the Ideal World. Here he calls it the life of that world or, in other words, the environment of God. It is true that we cannot speak of identification, but whatever difference there may be would necessarily be little more than a logical difference. Just as the νοῦς and the νοητά are actually one, and are distinguished only logically, so the concepts *God* and *eternity* are actually identical, and only logically distinguished. In the sense that eternity belongs to the essence of God, and that the Ideal World without eternity is unthinkable, we are entitled to speak of identity, but because there is a logical distinction, without actual separation, Plotinus is right when he says that we are not entitled to call the two concepts one. The one without the other is unthinkable, but because they represent two aspects of the same principle, we may speak of distinction without separation.

Plotinus stresses the essential connection between the Ideal World and the concept *eternity*. 'We must, however, avoid thinking of it as an accidental from outside grafted upon that nature. It is native to it, integral to it'.[349] In the same paragraph he explains that the Ideal World and everything in it must essentially belong to that concept. Eternity is eternally one with God in the same way as goodness is one with Him. For that very reason it is so impossible to speak of attributes of the Ideal World. If something belongs to the essence of an entity, it cannot be an attribute, because an attribute presupposes something subsidiary.

The next step in the argument of Plotinus is that God *is* not only eternal but that He could not be anything else. Here he gives the anology of things that have become and are continually in a state of becoming, on the one hand, and the things that have not become and that consequently cannot change or disappear. 'The essential existence of generated things seems to lie in their existing from the time of their generation to the ultimate of time after which they cease to be. But such existence is compact of futurity, and the annulment of that futurity means the stopping of the life and therefore of the essential existence.'[350] For that reason things that have come into being are continually in a process of further additions and the acquisition of additional attributes. When that process ceases, the existence of the entity ceases with it.

Over against that is the Ideal World. 'To an authentic All it is not enough that it be everything that exists; it must possess all-ness in the full sense that nothing whatever is absent from it. Then nothing is in store for it. If anything were to come, that thing must have been lacking to it, and it was, therefore, not All'.[351] The eternity of the eternal world is therefore presupposed by virtue of its perfection, and *vice versa*. Plotinus finds the perfection of the Ideal World not only in the perfection inherent in its different aspects, but also in its immunity from all lack, and by the exclusion of everything that does not fully participate in its being.[352] In other words, all communion with the created world is excluded, and *becoming* belongs to that world. *Becoming* is therefore excluded from the Ideal World, and consequently there is no past nor future.

According to Plotinus, the criterion that decides whether an entity is eternal, is to be found in the answer to the question whether it is essentially subject to change. If it is, that entity is not eternal. The question, let that be clear, is not whether a given entity actually does change. It must essentially be incapable of change. There is a vast difference between an eternal and a never-ending entity, in the same way as there is a difference between never-ending time and eternity.

In this sense eternity is nothing else than the life or the essence of God. Plotinus says: 'A close enough definition of eternity would be that it is a life limitless in the full sense of being all the life there is, and a life which, knowing nothing of past or future to shatter its completeness, possesses itself intact for ever. To the notion of a life all-comprehensive, add that it never spends itself, and we have the statement of a life instantaneously infinite'.[353]

In our discussion of the Plotinian concept *beauty*, we came to the conclusion that it leads to the concept *life* as the highest value. Here our conclusion is apparently similar. Eternity is the life of God, and time, as we shall see, is nothing more than the imperfect manifestation of that life, where, in the visible universe, it is forced to appear in intimate contact with matter. Eternity is the expression of the Ideal World as a true unity, not simply in the sense that it is

one, but also in the sense that it is essentially one, and that it never
can be anything else. Here we have another proof of the unity of the
three hypostases of the Ideal World. Plotinus says that 'Being can
have no this and that. It cannot be treated in terms of intervals,
unfoldings, progression, extension; there is no grasping any first or
last in it'.[354]

If there were a gradation in the Ideal World, there would not
have been that self-sufficient immutability that is a *conditio sine qua
non* for eternity. Plotinus even goes so far as to deny our right to
speak of the unity of the Ideal World, because that would presuppose the possibility of something else than unity. 'Being is self-
identical throughout and it is therefore one undistinguishable
thing'.[355] In the same way there is no difference between being and
eternal being.

# IX

# THE BASIS OF RELIGIOUS MYSTICISM

MYSTICISM is the practical application of idealistic thought. It has nothing to do with the pathological aberrations that are so often mistaken for religious ecstasy. This latter phenomenon is described in certain religious handbooks, and there we usually find an attempt to give precise rules of conduct necessary for the devotee who desires to practice mysticism, in other words, a *vade-mecum* or Baedeker's guide to communion with God. I have no wish to belittle works of this kind, but it must be made clear that it is a far cry indeed from this type of religious devotion to the Plotinian theory of religious mysticism. In the *Enneads* we will find little more than the practical application, in the field of religious devotion, of the results of philosophical thought.

The central thesis of the philosophy of Plotinus is the reality of an Ideal World that transcends our values, such as thought, virtue, beauty, and life; secondly, the existence, or rather pseudo-reality, of the visible universe; and thirdly, the continuity of the visible universe and the Ideal World. Furthermore, it must be remembered that Plotinus finds no place for conscious volition in the Ideal World, and consequently there is no possibility of a written revelation such as is found in Christianity, the Islam, and other religions.

Man, in his attempt to find God, is therefore constrained to seek Him in the highest divine manifestation, which, as we have already seen, is the human soul, or rather the intuitive phase of that soul. It can therefore be expected that Plotinus would be introspective in his religious practice, but his introspection will not, in the first place, be a subjective matter, because it has a metaphysical basis; and secondly, his religious practice will not be merely introspective.

Plotinus argues from the standpoint that not all men are capable of coming into conscious contact with God, and that those who are able to do so, cannot all follow the same road. 'In ourselves the relation to the Supreme is not identical from soul to soul; some of us are capable of becoming uniate, others of striving and almost attaining, while a third rank is much less apt. It is a matter of the degree or powers of the soul by which our expression is determined

—the first degree dominant in one person, the second, and the third in others, while all of us nevertheless contain all the powers'.[356]

In another *Ennead* the same thought is expressed in even more explicit terms. He says: 'But how lies the course? Is it alike for all, or is there a distinct method for each class of temperament? . . . We must begin by distinguishing these types'.[357]

With reference to the first thesis that not everyone is capable of finding God, there is the passage in *Ennead* v. 1, 1, where Plotinus points out that the soul can aggravate the inevitable consequences of its relationship to matter, to such a degree, that it can 'forget its father, God, and though a member of the Divine, and entirely of that world, to ignore at once itself and It'.[358] But even those materialistic souls are yet to a certain extent capable of improving. 'Anyone not of the strength to lay hold of the first soul, that possessing intellection, must grasp that which has to do with our ordinary thinking, and thence proceed. . . . One may even, if it seem necessary, begin as low as the reproductive soul and thence make the ascent'.[359]

This is a very important concession, and it wholly disproves the standpoint of those scholars who find in the religion of Plotinus nothing more than an irrational or even supra-rational ecstasy. It is true that the intuitive phase of the soul transcends the reasoning faculty, and that the road to God that leads through the intuitive phase must be the road of ecstasy, but this passage tells us that the road of ecstasy, although it is the most direct road, is not the only one.

In this respect there is, therefore, a fundamental difference between the religious mysticism of Plotinus and the orientally inspired mystery religions of the Hellenistic world, where the mystic is regarded as a person who, by virtue of a revealed knowledge of God, is brought into contact with the Supreme. There is very little force in Brehier's argument that Plotinus is an Oriental mystic more than a Greek philosopher.[360] One of Brehier's strongest arguments is based on the passage in the *Enneads* where Plotinus says that, if man desires to see God 'all the need is met by a purely intellective contact. At the moment of touch there is no power whatever to make any affirmation; there is no leisure; reasoning upon the vision is for afterwards'.[361]

But this passage gives no indication whatsoever of Oriental leanings in Plotinus. There is a vast difference between the 'intellective contact' [νοερῶς ἐφάψασθαι] and the Nirvana of the twice-born

Yogi. What exactly is the meaning of νοερῶς and νόησις? I have, as a rule, adopted the translation of Mackenna of *intellective*, but, as has already been said, it denotes a function of the soul that transcends the ordinary discursive reasoning of man, because it makes no use of the ordinary inductive and deductive methods of thought. It is therefore not sub-rational, but supra-rational, and certainly not irrational. In the second place, according to Plotinus, the attitude in which such *intellection* can be practised can only be reached by a preparatory use of the discursive reason, or διάνοια, a condition certainly not demanded by Nirvana. And in the third place Plotinus makes it clear that the products of νόησις are ultimately capable of control by the discursive reason.

We have already seen that Plotinus does not prescribe the same road to all seekers after God.[362] But there is one limitation. In *Ennead* I. 3 he deals with dialectics or, as he calls it, the upward road, where the goal is God. He distinguishes three types of pilgrims on that road, but for all there are two essential preliminary steps. 'The first degree is the conversion from the lower life; the second, held by those that have already made their way to the sphere of the Intelligibles, have set as it were a footprint there, but must still advance within the realm, and it lasts until they reach the extreme hold of the place, the term attained when the topmost peak of the realm is won'.[363]

Of the first step we need not say much at this stage. It is the *katharsis* of which we have already spoken in our discussion of the ethics of Plotinus. Here he mentions the different methods by which this *katharsis* or purification must be effected, and he explains the threefold way of the philosopher, the lover and the musician.

A brief comment on this threefold way would be instructive. It will be remembered that in our treatment of the metaphysics, the aesthetics and the ethics of Plotinus the final conclusion in every case was that God, or the Ideal World, was at the summit of these values, and that, in that world, these three values were found to be one. To say that God could be found along the threefold way of the philosopher, the lover and the musician, is merely to say that the search for God leads along the way of truth, of goodness and of beauty. Those three values are manifestations of one God, and in their essence they are identical. By reason of the limitations of our time-space reason we see them as three distinct values, but a progressive search in any one of them, will reveal God.

By nature we are better fitted for one road than for another. The one man is by nature a philosopher, the other a moralist, the third a lover of beauty. Let each of those three seek to find God along the upward way of his own particular predilection, and the outcome is the same. God is revealed as the transcendent source of what is true, of what is beautiful, and of what is good.

Of the musicians he says the following: 'The musician we may think of as being exceedingly quick to beauty, drawn in a very rapture to it; somewhat slow to stir of his own impulse, he answers at once to the outer stimulus. As the timid are sensitive to noise, so he to tones and the beauty they convey; all that offends against unison or harmony in melodies or rhythms repels him; he longs for measure and shapely pattern'.[364] From his natural urge for beauty, a person of this type must attempt to reach the concept of an all-transcending beauty that is the source of all beauty in the time-space world. 'He must be shown that what has ravished him was no other than the harmony of the Intellectual world, and the beauty in that sphere—not some one shape of beauty, but the All-Beauty, the Absolute Beauty'.[365]

In a later tractate Plotinus discusses this matter more fully. He points out that the beauty of God is inaccessible, and that the seeker must turn away from the beauty of visible and audible things, and 'withdraw into himself'.[366] The initial introspection will not yield a full vision. The manifestation will be gradual. In the first place the beauty of beautiful actions must be contemplated, then the beauty of lives and of characters, and only then the beauty of human souls. And then comes his climax. Knowledge can ultimately come only by similarity. To love beauty, the lover must himself be beautiful. 'Therefore, first let each become godlike and each beautiful who cares to see God and beauty'.[367]

The same rules apply, *mutatis mutandis*, in the case of the lover. 'The born lover has a certain memory of beauty but, severed from it now, he no longer comprehends it . . . He must be led, under a system of mental discipline, to beauty everywhere, and made to discern the one principle underlying all, a principle apart from material forms, springing from another source. . . . From the virtues he is to be lead to the Intellectual Principle'.[368] Of the third class, the philosopher, Plotinus has very little to say. He has a higher rank than the others. 'He needs only a guide'.[369] The only practical direction to the philosopher is a course in mathematics to train him in abstract thought, and in a faith in the unembodied.

So much for the difference between the three types. From this point onwards the roads again become one. After the preliminary process of purification, philosopher and lover and musician must practice the science of dialectics which Plotinus describes as 'the method or discipline that brings with it the power of pronouncing with final truth upon the nature and relation of things—what each is, how it differs from the others, what common quality all have, to what kind each belongs and in what rank each stands in its kind, and whether its being is real being, and how many beings there are and how many non-beings to be distinguished from beings'.[370]

Nor is this all. Dialectics, according to Plotinus, is nothing less than philosophy in its widest definition. The seeker after God will, therefore, after his purification from the taint of his association with the material world, seek in the realm of unembodied concepts, and there find the eternal values.

And only then is the practice of pure religion possible. The human reason is the agent in the act of dialectics, and religion consists of the enjoyment of the fruits of that act. This enjoyment he calls intellection or νόησις—itself not an act of the discursive reason, but nevertheless made possible only by reason of the fact that the discursive reason, by a preliminary act, had cleared the ground and had enabled the soul to contemplate God without the obscuring influence of the material world.

'Now the soul rests. Instructed and satisfied as to the Being in that sphere, it is no longer busy about many things; it has arrived at Unity and it contemplates; it leaves to another science all that coil of premises and conclusions called the art of reasoning, much as it leaves the art of writing. Some of the matter of logic, no doubt, it considers necessary, to clear the ground, but it makes itself the judge, here as in everything else; where it sees use, it uses; anything it finds superfluous, it leaves to whatever department of learning or practice may turn that matter to account'.[371]

The mystical contemplation of Plotinus is therefore the result of rational thought, and, furthermore, there is a measure of logic retained in the very act of contemplation itself. It does not, like Oriental mysticism, despise the different departments of logical science, but, on the contrary, it allows those sciences to deal each with its own appropriate data. What Plotinus says in this tractate is virtually the following: 'With my reason I find God. After I have found Him, I have not the same need of my reason as previously. God can be found by means of the laws of logic, but those laws cannot analyse Him. The power and indispensability of logic are freely granted, but in the case of a simplex it is powerless, because its only function is to analyse, and a simplex is incapable of analysis. After I have reached the Simplex, by the power of my reason, I contemplate that Simplex, because there is nothing else left for me to do'. Even mystical contemplation, the act of ἐν ἡσυχία βλέπειν, has its laws, based on the nature of the Ideal World.[372] In other words, the nature of contemplation is determined by the nature of God.

Two questions remain to be answered in connection with the religious mysticism of Plotinus. The first is the basic justification for contemplation, and the second is the way in which that contemplation or mystic union takes place.

With reference to the first question we will remember that Plotinus postulates the immanence of the Ideal World in all entities. Everything is therefore ensouled, in the sense of the immanence of the formative Soul as hypostasis of the Ideal World. It will also be remembered that Plotinus finds no place in his system for a supernatural revelation of the Ideal World. The visible universe is therefore the only revelation of God at our disposal. The manifestation of that world in the different entities of the universe differs in degree, according to the measure in which matter or idea predominates in those entities. It is the task of philosophy, with logic as its instrument, to reach the unity of God inductively, with the multiplicity of entities as preliminary data. The highest unity, and consequently the purest manifestation of God, is the human soul. God is a universal concept, and can therefore not be at a particular time and place in his totality. To find God, we must therefore go to that entity in which the highest divine manifestation is to be found, and that entity is the human soul. Consequently that final search, which takes the form of contemplation, will be introspective. It therefore follows logically from the system of Plotinus that man must turn to himself to find God.

The second question brings us back to the *Enneads*. The premise here is that man is in direct contact with God, and that there are therefore no limitations of time and space in connection with contemplation. 'The souls of men, seeing their images in the mirror of Dionysus, as it were, have entered into that realm in a leap downward from the Supreme. Yet even they are not yet cut off from their origin, from the divine Intellect. It is not that they have come bringing the Intellectual Principle down in their fall. It is that though they have descended even to earth, yet their higher part holds for ever above the heavens'.[373]

In other words, the source from which the soul has sprung, remains its true home. By virtue of the divine origin of the soul, the worshipper is always in immediate contact with God, and akin to this is the truth that 'the All must, in every detail of act and experience, be an expression of the Supreme'.[374] The human soul is the fount where knowledge of God may be acquired, not because God cannot be known at any other place or in any other way, but because, in the human soul, He is revealed in a fuller degree than in other entities. For Plotinus, as for the poet of the Psalms, 'the heavens declare the glory of God, and the firmament showeth his handiwork'. Like the banished duke in the forest of Arden, he 'finds tongues in trees, books in the running brooks, sermons in stones, and' to improve upon Shakespeare, 'God in everything'.

How is that mystical union to be effected? 'One certain way to this knowledge is to separate first the man from the body—yourself, that is, from your body—next to put aside that soul which moulded the body, and, very earnestly, the system of sense with desires and impulses and every such futility, all setting definitely towards the mortal; what is left is the phase of the soul which we have declared to be an image of the divine Intellect'.[375] Although he calls it here the image of the divine Intellect, in other words, of the Intellectual Principle, he says in the same tractate that that aspect or phase of the soul is in the closest touch with God, not in transit, but centred there.

The purification of which Plotinus speaks here is explained by him in another tractate. In the first place there is the recognition by the soul of its own value. It must realize that it is nearer to God than the visible universe.

'This, by which the gods [the stars] are divine, must be the oldest god of them all. And our own soul is of that same ideal nature, so that to consider it, purified, freed from all accruement, is to recognize in ourselves that same value which we have found soul to be, honourable above all that is bodily'.[376]

After this purification, man becomes one with God, or, to put it differently, man realizes his unity with God. Man must put into practice the theory of the immanence of God. 'A man becomes Intellectual Principle when, ignoring all other phases of his being, he sees through that only and so knows himself by means of the self—in other words, attains the self-knowledge which the Intellectual Principle possesses'.[377] And the person who has attained that knowledge of himself or of God, becomes the initiated, who is qualified to practice communion with God.

Plotinus tells us that he often practised such communion. 'Many times it has happened. Lifted out of the body into myself; becoming external to all other things and self-centred; beholding a marvellous beauty; then, more than ever, assured of community with the loftiest order; enacting the noblest life, acquiring identity with the divine; . . . yet, there comes the moment of descent from intellection to reasoning, and after that sojourn in the divine, I ask myself how it happens that I can now be descending, and how did the soul ever enter into my body, the soul which, even within the body, is the high thing it has shown itself to be'.[378]

Here we have pure religious ecstasy, if, at least, we may use that word of an activity that is purely introspective. One can describe it as an overwhelming realization of one's own divinity, and the renunciation of everything that can possibly obscure that divinity. And it means that matter and all its associations must be renounced, because it is through the agency of matter that the divine element in man is obscured. That means that not only embodiment must as far as possible be neutralized, but even the rational soul must be kept in abeyance, because it is the organ of the *soul-as-using-body*, that composite entity that we have called the living conjoint. 'The very soul, once it has conceived the straining love towards this, lays aside all the shape it has taken, even to the intellectual shape that has informed it. The soul must see before it neither evil nor good nor anything else, that alone it may receive the Alone'.[379]

This is perfectly in accord with the Plotinian theory of the being of God. He has no attribute[380] and He cannot be named.[381] Before approaching Him, man also must be relieved of all his addenda, all attributes. Everything must be cut away, and the pure man, in other words, the divine phase of the soul, alone must remain.[382]

And because that pure man is no longer in any relation to matter, man in that state will no longer be an ethical being, because the ethical quality of an entity is a result of its dual relationship to matter and to God. The categories of good and evil, like all other categories, except those which are related to the Ideal World, will not be applicable. In other words, in the moment of ecstasy, man himself is God.

Inge[383] says that 'this vision of the One is no part of the philosophy of Plotinus, but a mischievous accretion. For . . . we cannot make it an object of sense'. But surely Plotinus makes it perfectly clear that the contemplation of the One is not a matter for the senses. The vision of which he speaks is a visible vision, not an object of the eyes! In the passage cited Plotinus says that the soul lays aside even the intellectual shape that has informed it. In other words, even the rational soul, the human reason, is left in abeyance, although it is by that reason that the soul has reached the conclusion that the contemplation of the Ideal World is its true function.

And this contemplation is not actually a function. It is no more than the acceptance by the soul of the fact that it is one with God. 'My soul waiteth upon God', we read in the Psalms. Far from being a function of the senses, it is that condition where not only the senses, but also the reasoning faculty, is suspended. Contemplation presupposes identity with the object of contemplation. It is therefore more a condition than an act. Human vision sees its own object as something apart. The religious ecstasy of Plotinus is the confession of one-ness with God.

# NOTES

With the references to the *Enneads* I give in brackets an indication of the page and line where the passage referred to may be found in the appropriate volume of R. Volkmann's edition of Plotinus (*Plotini Enneades edidit Ricardus Volkmann*, Vols. I. & II., Leipzig, 1884).

[1] III. 6, 13 (161, 1–5).
[2] v. 1, 1 (162, 12–17).
[3] v. 1, 1 (162, 1–5).
[4] v. 1, 1 (162, 1–5).
[5] v. 1, 3 (164, 12–17).
[6] v. 3, 12 (194, 15–22).
[7] v. 3, 5 (183, 9–11; 184, 1–3).
[8] v. 5, 6 (213, 21–22; 24–29. See also v. 3, 14).
[9] Leighton, *Man and the Cosmos*, Appleton, 1922, pp. 495–500.
[10] v. 5, 4 (210, 25–30).
[11] VI. 9, 2 (509, 23–24).
[12] VI. 9, 3 (510, 24—511, 7).
[13] Cf. Whittaker, *The Neoplatonists*, Cambridge, 1928, p. 57.
[14] Cf. v. 3, 16 and 17.
[15] v. 3, 13 (196, 3–12).
[16] VI. 4, 2 (363, 18–21; 364, 15–20).
[17] III. 9, 3 (349, 3–5).
[18] v. 3, 14 (197, 13–15).
[19] Caird, *The Evolution of Theology in the Greek Philosophers*, Glasgow, 1923, Vol. 2, p. 220.
[20] v. 3, 14 (197, 16–17; 21–24; 198, 1–2).
[21] v. 3, 17 (202, 1–14).
[22] v. 5, 6 (212, 28—213, 3).
[23] v. 3, 13 (196, 13–14; 21–23; 26–27; 29–31).
[24] v. 6, 4 (225, 9–12).
[25] v. 6, 5 (226, 2–6; 9–10; 11–12; 14–15).
[26] Inge, *The Philosophy of Plotinus*, Longmans, 1918, Vol. II., p. 114.
[27] Eucken, *Lebensanschauungen d. grosser Denker*, Berlin, 1930, pp. 124–7.
[28] VI. 8, 2 (479, 28–32).
[29] VI. 8, 4 (482, 3–9).
[30] v. 6, 5 (226, 3–7; 11–12; 14–15).
[31] VI. 8, 7 (486, 11–16; 17–22; 487, 5–9).
[32] VI. 8, 11 (492, 8—493, 14).
[33] VI. 8, 8 (488, 3–9).
[34] VI. 9, 6 (516, 32—517, 5).
[35] II. 9, 1 (184, 4–9).
[36] VI. 9, 6 (517, 9–13).
[37] Caird, *op. cit.*, Vol. II, pp. 240–2.
[38] Grandgeorge, *Augustin et le Neoplatonisme*, Paris, 1896, p. 119.
[39] Eucken, *op. cit.*, pp. 124–7.
[40] Inge, *op. cit.*, Vol. II, p. 114.
[41] Leighton, *op. cit.*, pp. 119–129.
[42] v. 3, 13 (196, 3–8).
[43] v. 5, 9 (216, 12–15; 17–20; 24–28).
[44] The Library of Philosophical Translations, *Plotinus*, translated by Stephen Mackenna, Med. Soc. Ltd., London, 1926.
[45] VI. 5, 9 (393, 16–19).
[46] v. 3, 12 (194, 15–16; 20–22).
[47] Stace, *A Critical History of Greek Philosophy*, Macmillan, 1924, p. 197.
[48] Inge, *op. cit.*, Vol. II., p. 82.
[49] v. 3, 12 (194, 20–22).

[50] v. 3, 14–15 (197, 16–17; 21–22; 198, 1–199, 2; 7–8).
[51] Inge, *op. cit.*, Vol. II, p. 82.
[52] v. 3, 8 (187, 30—188, 4).
[53] v. 9, 9–10 (256, 6–11; 21–28; 31–32).
[54] v. 9, 10 (257, 9–12).
[55] v. 9, 14 (259, 21–26; 30–31).
[56] v. 1, 4 (165, 10–19; 20–22; 27–28; 31—166, 3; 166, 7–9).
[57] v. 3, 6 (185, 11–14. I translate πειθώ by *discursive knowledge* and ἀνάγκη by *immediate knowledge*. That, I think, is the meaning.)
[58] v. 6, 1 (222, 28—223, 8).
[59] vi. 2, 4 (303, 30—304, 11).
[60] vi. 2, 4 (304, 17–18).
[61] vi. 2, 5 (305, 6–10).
[62] vi. 2, 5 (305, 16–17).
[63] vi. 2, 5 (305, 20).
[64] vi. 2, 7 (307, 32—308, 1).
[65] vi. 2, 7 (308, 13–17).
[66] vi. 2, 8 (308, 31–32).
[67] vi. 2, 8 (309, 27–28).
[68] Zeller, *Plato and the Older Academy*, translated by Alleyne and Goodwin, Longmans p. 226.
[69] Inge, *op. cit.*, Vol. II., p. 58.
[70] Turner, *The Philosophic Basis of Moral Obligation*, p. 37.
[71] v. 3, 10 (191, 16—192, 28).
[72] v. 3, 5 (183, 9–11; 184, 1–3).
[73] iii. 8, 4 (334, 23–25; 27—335, 6).
[74] v. 3, 3–4 (181, 22–27; 182, 3–8).
[75] v. 3, 5 (183, 25—184, 7).
[76] Inge, *op. cit.*, Vol. II., p. 77.
[77] v. 8.
[78] v. 8, 3 (234, 1–7; 11).
[79] v. 3, 3 (180, 17–30).
[80] v. 8, 7 (238, 31—239, 9; 12–13; 14–19; 27–28).
[81] v. 9, 4 (251, 24–29).
[82] v. 8, 10 (244, 19–24).
[83] v. 9, 10 (256, 21–23; 257, 9–12).
[84] v. 8, 11 (244, 25–31).
[85] v. 1, 6 (167, 19–28; 168, 3–18; 30–169, 11).
[86] v. 3, 6–7 (186, 6–27).
[87] v. 8, 8 (340, 10–11).
[88] v. 8, 1 (230, 24–27).
[89] iii. 2, 14.
[90] iii. 8, 10 (344, 16–22).
[91] ψυχή can therefore be one of the following: (i) the third hypostasis of the Godhead; (ii) the Soul of the Universe; (iii) the particular soul, either in its vegetative, its discursive-rational, or religious-intuitive phase.
[92] v. 2, 1 (176, 19–22).
[93] v. 1, 3 (164, 13–23; 30–31).
[94] iii. 8, 10 (343, 27—344, 1).
[95] v. 1, 6 (168, 8–10; 16–18).
[96] v. 1, 2 (162, 18–28; 163, 7–13; 16–24).
[97] iii. 7, 11 (325, 9–14; 18–22; 25–29).
[98] *Historia Philosophiae Gracae et Romanae ex fontium locis contexta*, Gotha, 1913.
[99] iii. 6, 18 (307, 15–16).
[100] iii. 7, 11 quoted above.
[101] iv. 8, 8 (152, 18–20).
[102] iv. 3, 12 (25, 15–18).
[103] iv. 3, 11 (23, 32—24, 1).
[104] v. 5, 9 (216, 12–17).
[105] Ἐπισκέψεις διάφοροι

[106] III. 9, 1 (347, 7–31).
[107] III. 9, 1 (346, 19–21).
[108] III. 9, 1 (quoted under [106] above).
[109] IV. 4, 2 (49, 11–22).
[110] Mackenna, *op. cit.*, Vol. I., p. 121.
[111] IV. 4, 9 (55, 24–30).
[112] IV. 4, 10 (55, 31—56, 9).
[113] IV. 7, 12 (327, 25–26).
[114] IV. 4, 10 and III. 9, 1.
[115] IV. 4, 16 (62, 17).
[116] IV. 4, 13 (60, 16–19).
[117] IV. 4, 15 (61, 14–22).
[118] IV. 4, 16 (61, 26—62, 14; 16–18).
[119] III. 2, 1 (225, 27—226, 3).
[120] II. 9.
[121] Inge, *op. cit.*, Vol. I., p. 108.
[122] III. 2, 1 (226, 20–28).
[123] Inge, *op. cit.*, Vol. I., pp. 143–4).
[124] III. 2, 1–2 (227, 16–18; 27–28).
[125] Inge, *op. cit.*, Vol. I., p. 145.
[126] Arnou, Πρᾶξις et θεωρία, Paris, 1921, p. 11.
[127] Proclus, *In Tim.*, 49.
[128] Inge, *op. cit.*, Vol. I, p. 145
[129] Cf. Dreas, *Die Usia bei Plotin*, Leipzig, 1912, p. 32.
[130] Zeller, *Geschichte d. Philosophie d. Griechen*, 1881, Vol. I., p. 506.
[131] III. 2, 16 (246, 11–15).
[132] III. 2, 17 (250, 4–6; 10–11).
[133] II. 9.
[134] II. 9, 4 (188, 18–22).
[135] II. 9, 5 (189, 4–6).
[136] II. 9, 5 (189, 17–20).
[137] II. 9, 5 (189, 23–28).
[138] Inge, *op. cit.*, Vol. I., p. 104.
[139] II. 9, 7 (192, 22–25).
[140] II. 9, 8.
[141] Whittaker, *The Neoplatonists*, Cambridge, p. 51.
[142] Inge, *op. cit.*, Vol. I., p. 106.
[143] II. 9, 9 (196, 30–32).
[144] II. 9, 16 (206, 17–19; 27–30).
[145] Mackenna, *op. cit.*, *Ethical Treatises*, p. 121.
[146] III. 2, 3 and III. 2, 12.
[147] IV. 4, 40–41 (95, 24–28; 30–96, 9).
[148] Cf. Turner, *op. cit.*, p. 65.
[149] II. 3, 1 (133, 16–21; 134, 2–5).
[150] II. 3, 1.
[151] II. 3, 3 (135, 24–28; 136, 6–8).
[152] Emile Brehier, *La Philosophie de Plotin*, Paris, 1928, pp. 107–135.
[153] II. 3, 1 (133, 11–14).
[154] II. 3, 7 (139, 17–21).
[155] II. 3, 8 (140, 9–10).
[156] Stace, *op. cit.*, p. 342.
[157] IV. 7, 1.
[158] IV. 7, 1 (121, 19–21).
[159] IV. 7, 3 (121, 29—122, 3).
[160] IV. 7, 3 (122, 5–8).
[161] IV. 7, 3 (122, 13–14).
[162] IV. 7, 3 (122, 14–17).
[163] Cf. Whittaker, *op. cit.*, p. 222.
[164] IV. 7, 6 (126, 14–19).
[165] IV. 7, 7 (128, 32—129, 1).

[166] IV. 3, 1.
[167] IV. 3, 2 (10, 18–19).
[168] IV. 3, 2.
[169] IV. 3, 3 (12, 26–28).
[170] IV. 9, 1 (153, 5–8).
[171] I. 1, 2. Cf. Kristeller, *Der Begriff der Seele in d. Ethik d. Plotins*, Tubingen, 1929, p. 12.
[172] I. 1, 2 (40, 19–20).
[173] I. 1, 3 (40, 28).
[174] IV. 2, 1 (4, 17; 23—5, 1).
[175] IV. 2, 1.
[176] Inge, *op. cit.*, Vol. I, p. 214.
[177] IV. 9, 2 (153, 31—154, 2).
[178] III. 1, 8 (224, 2–7).
[179] VI. 5, 7 (389, 31—390, 4).
[180] IV. 3, 2 (12, 1–7).
[181] IV. 3, 3 (12, 29—13, 5).
[182] IV. 3, 6 (16, 11–12). Cf. Kristeller, *op. cit.*, p. 94, who says that soul is merely one of the causes of the cosmos, and that failure to create is due to the absence of other causes. But Plotinus knows nothing of it.
[183] Inge, *op. cit.*, Vol. I, pp. 205–13.
[184] IV. 3, 4 (14, 4–8).
[185] II. 9, 5 (188, 30—189, 6).
[186] IV. 3, 6 (15, 21–23; 16, 11–12).
[187] V. 3, 9 (190, 1–8).
[188] IV. 3, 12 (24, 14–19).
[189] IV. 7, 10 (138, 11–27).
[190] Plato, *Phaedrus*, 246.
[191] Plato, *Georg.*, 523.
[192] Inge, *op. cit.*, Vol. II., p. 8.
[193] Cf. *Phaedrus* 76, where he speaks of a series of lives.
[194] Cf. Davidson, *The Stoic Creed*, p. 96.
[195] Origen, *In Psalmos*, 533.
[196] II. 9, 8.
[197] IV. 7, 11 (139, 10–11).
[198] IV. 7, 15 (141, 28—142, 8).
[199] IV. 4, 29 (78, 27–29; 30–32; 79, 1; 7–8; 12; 27–29).
[200] Cf. III. 6, 6.
[201] IV. 4, 1 (47, 11–22).
[202] IV. 4, 2 (48, 19–25).
[203] IV. 4, 2 (49, 11–19).
[204] IV. 4, 4 (50, 15–17).
[205] IV. 4, 2 (49, 21–22).
[206] Heineman, *Plotin*, Leipzig, 1921, p. 280.
[207] V. 5, 1 (206, 16–25).
[208] V. 9, 7 (254, 20–23).
[209] IV. 3, 6 (16, 20–21; 23–25).
[210] Inge, *op. cit.*, Vol. II, p. 31.
[211] Inge, *op. cit.*, Vol. II., p. 33.
[212] IV. 4, 1.
[213] Probably the *Phaedo*.
[214] III. 4, 6 (265, 15–19).
[215] IV. 4, 6–7 (52, 3–5; 9–13; 17–23).
[216] Inge, *op. cit.*, Vol. I., p. 221.
[217] IV. 4, 29 (see above).
[218] The most important passages in this connection are IV. 4; IV. 3; IV. 6; III. 6; I. 1; V. 5 and VI. 7.
[219] IV. 4, 23 (70, 16–22).
[220] IV. 4, 23.
[221] IV. 3, 23.
[222] IV. 3, 23 (35, 31—36, 5).

M

[223] IV. 5, 1 (102, 13–19).
[224] IV. 5, 1.
[225] e.g. I. 1, 11; IV. 4, 40; IV. 5, 3.
[226] IV. 6, 2 (116, 9–12).
[227] IV. 6, 2 (116, 29–31).
[228] IV. 6, 3 (117, 10–13).
[229] IV. 6, 3 (117, 16–17).
[230] IV. 6, 3 (117, 22–28).
[231] IV. 6, 3 (118, 20–23).
[232] IV. 3, 25–27.
[233] IV. 3, 25 (39, 6–9).
[234] Inge, *op. cit.*, Vol. I., p. 227.
[235] IV. 3, 26.
[236] Ficinus, *Mars. Argumentum*, Vol. II., p. 730.
[237] IV. 3, 25.
[238] IV. 3, 26.
[239] V. 5, 3.
[240] IV. 4, 18.
[241] Inge, *op. cit.*, Vol. I., p. 225.
[242] IV. 4, 20
[243] V. 4, 20 (67, 8–12).
[244] IV. 4, 20 (67, 27–31).
[245] IV. 4, 20.
[246] Caird, *The Evolution of Theology in the Greek Philosophers*, Glasgow, 1923, pp. 220–221.
[247] Leighton, *op. cit.*, p. 51.
[248] V. 3, 2–3.
[249] V. 3, 3 (180, 17–19).
[250] V. 3, 3 (180, 18–27).
[251] Cf. Bosanquet, *Logic*, Vol. II., ch. 9–10.
[252] Joachim, *The Nature of Truth*, p. 72.
[253] Leighton, *op. cit.*, p. 53.
[254] V. 5, 1 (206, 16–25).
[255] V. 5, 2.
[256] V. 5, 2.
[257] V. 6, 3.
[258] I. 6, 9 (95, 15–20; 22–23).
[259] I. 6, 5 (90, 18–24).
[260] I. 6, 5 (90, 24–30).
[261] I. 6, 5 (91, 12–14; 18–24).
[262] III. 6, 2.
[263] III. 6, 7 (291, 16—292, 3).
[264] III. 6, 9 (293, 27–28).
[265] III. 6, 9 (294, 7–13).
[266] III. 6, 10 (295, 19–22).
[267] III. 6, 11 (297, 4–6).
[268] III. 6, 13 (300, 32—301, 8).
[269] III. 6, 16 (304, 11–14; 305, 6–10).
[270] III. 6, 18.
[271] I. 8, 1 (99, 12–19).
[272] I. 8, 2.
[273] I. 8, 3 (101, 31—102, 2; 6–17).
[274] I. 8, 4.
[275] I. 8, 4 (102, 30–103, 11).
[276] I. 8, 5 (103, 26–32; 104, 2–4).
[277] I. 8, 5 (104, 4–5).
[278] III. 1, 2 (216, 18–21).
[279] III. 1, 2 (216, 18–21).
[280] III. 1, 2 (217, 1–2).
[281] III. 1, 4.
[282] III. 1, 9.

[283] III. 1, 10 (225, 9–25).
[284] I. 8, 5 (104, 5–8).
[285] I. 8, 5.
[286] I. 8, 5 (104, 14–19).
[287] I. 8, 5 (104, 19–24).
[288] I. 8, 6 (105, 7–9).
[289] I. 8, 7.
[290] I. 8, 8 (109, 3–10).
[291] I. 8, 9 (109, 18–21).
[292] Schröder, *Plotin, Abhandlung* πόθεν τὰ κακά, Leipzig, 1916.
[293] Caird, *op. cit.*, Vol. II.
[294] Inge, *op. cit.*, Vol. I., p. 143.
[295] II. 9, 8.
[296] Turner, *The Philosophic Basis of Moral Obligation*, Macmillan, 1924.
[297] Turner, *op. cit.*, p. 271.
[298] V. 5, 6 (212, 28—213, 3).
[299] I. 2, 1 (51, 13–20).
[300] V. 3, 11 (193, 30–32).
[301] III. 6, 9–10 (295, 4–5; 21–22).
[302] I. 8.
[303] I. 8, 8 (109, 3–10).
[304] I. 1, 9 (46, 1–3).
[305] I. 1, 9 (46, 13–17).
[306] I. 1, 9 (46, 6–8; 11).
[307] I. 2, 4 (54, 6–10).
[308] I. 2, 4.
[309] I. 2, 4.
[310] I. 2, 5 (54, 31–55, 13).
[311] Cf. Whittaker, *op. cit.*, who says that Plotinus is dominated by asceticism.
[312] Inge, *op. cit.*, Vol. I., pp. 25–27.
[313] Porphyrius, *Vita Plotini*. 12.
[314] I. 3, 6 (62, 6–10).
[315] I. 2, 1 (51, 13–19).
[316] I., 2, 1.
[317] I. 2, 2 (52, 4–6).
[318] I. 2, 2 (52, 12–13).
[319] I. 2, 2 (52, 26–27).
[320] I. 2, 3.
[321] I. 2, 3.
[322] I. 2, 3 (52, 32–53, 4).
[323] Porphyrius, *Vita Plotini*, 1.
[324] Inge, *op. cit.*, Vol. II., p. 176. Inge says that the Plotinian purification is the practice of the civic virtues, with duty instead of habit as the motive. I have found no trace of this distinction in Plotinus.
[325] III. 6, 5 (288, 6–9).
[326] I. 6, 8 (95, 2–7).
[327] I. 6, 9 (95, 16–22).
[328] I. 6, and V. 8.
[329] I. 6, 1 (85, 1–2).
[330] *Poetics*, 4.
[331] I. 6, 2 (86, 28–32).
[332] I. 6, 3 (87, 27–30).
[333] I. 6, 5 (89, 24–31; 90, 8–9; 10–11).
[334] Inge, *op. cit.*, Vol. II., p. 216.
[335] I. 6, 5 (90, 24–30).
[336] V. 8, 1.
[337] *Poetics*, 11.
[338] *Poetics*, 11.
[339] V. 8, 1.
[340] Inge, *op. cit.*, Vol. II., p. 214.

341 v. 8, 2 (233, 27–30).
342 III. 7, 1.
343 III. 7, 2.
344 III. 7, 2 (312, 3–11).
345 III. 7, 2.
346 III. 7, 2.
347 III. 7, 3 (312, 20–22).
348 III. 7, 3 (313, 6–11).
349 III. 7, 4 (313, 12–14).
350 III. 7, 4 (314, 6–11).
351 III. 7, 4 (313, 25–28).
352 III. 7, 3.
353 III. 7, 5 (315, 24–30).
354 III. 7, 6 (316, 14–16).
355 III. 7, 6 (316, 13–14).
356 IV, 3, 6 (16, 22–28).
357 I. 3, 1 (58, 9–10; 18–20).
358 v. 1, 1 (161, 2–5).
359 v. 3, 9 (190, 30–191, 1; 191, 4–5).
360 Brehier, *op. cit.*, pp. 106–133.
361 v. 3, 17
362 I. 3, 1.
363 I. 3, 1.
364 I. 3, 1.
365 I. 3, 1.
366 I. 6, 8
367 I. 6, 9 (96, 12–14).
368 I. 3, 2 (59, 6; 8–9; 11–14; 19–20).
369 I. 3, 3 (59, 22 . . . 25).
370 I. 3, 4 (60, 2–6).
371 I. 3, 4 (60, 19–26).
372 I. 3, 3.
373 IV., 3, 12 (24, 14–19).
374 IV., 312 (25, 10–12).
375 v. 3, 9 (190, 1–8).
376 v. 1, 2 (164, 2–7).
377 v. 3, 4 (183, 5–8).
378 IV. 8, 1 (142, 10–15; 17–21).
379 VI. 7, 34 (466, 21–27).
380 v. 5, 6.
381 v. 3, 14.
382 v. 4, 17.
383 Inge, *Christian Mysticism*, Methuen, 1925, p. 96.

# INDEX